How ha
undermining our law and society

How hate crime policy is undermining our law and society

Richard Norrie

CIVITAS

First published
May 2021

© Civitas 2021

55 Tufton Street
London SW1P 3QL

email: books@civitas.org.uk

ISBN 978-1-912581-25-2

Independence: Civitas: Institute for the Study of Civil
Society is a registered educational charity (No. 1085494)
and a company limited by guarantee (No. 04023541).
Civitas is financed from a variety of private sources to
avoid over-reliance on any single or small group of donors.

All the Institute's publications seek to further its objective
of promoting the advancement of learning. The views
expressed are those of the authors, not of the Institute.

Typeset by Typetechnique

Printed in Great Britain
by 4edge Limited, Essex

Contents

Author

Richard Norrie is Director of the Statistics and Policy Research Programme at Civitas.

Summary

- This report offers a critical appraisal of the ideas behind what we call 'hate crime' as well as the evidence for it. While crime motivated by hatred is to be condemned, as is all crime, we have ushered in a response to it that is corrosive.

- It is argued that we have entered into a new way of doing law, that sees thought as something to be punished where it leads to crime. This can be objected to on liberal principle.

- Hate crime legislation has been introduced in a piecemeal fashion. It can be traced back to legal attempts to stifle fascism, and to penalise the incitement to violence. However, it has changed its nature and now stands for the punishment of offensive ideas, as well as greater penalty for crimes committed against people with some characteristics but not all characteristics. It has thus introduced inequality before the law.

- The innovation in hate crime legislation can be traced to the 1997 Labour Party Manifesto, off the back of which was introduced racially and subsequently religiously aggravated offences. The consequence of this has been that more advocacy groups have lobbied for the inclusion of their own favoured characteristics.

- The state pumps out statistics on the numbers of hate crimes, giving precedence to those recorded by police. These numbers fuel stories of a rising tide of hatred, widely promulgated in a credulous media.

- But no serious criminologist would ever infer a rising trend from police recorded figures which do not have the status of 'national statistics'. This is because they are subject to the willingness to report as well as political direction.

- As noted by the Commission on Race and Ethnic Disparities, the more reliable data taken from the Crime Survey of England and Wales points to a decline in hate crime overall.

- The Government has made it a priority to tackle hate crime despite acknowledging it to be declining. It is official policy to 'get the numbers up', meaning the state is actively encouraging reporting.

- What this has led to is the police prioritising crimes which are relatively trivial and may not even be crimes at all. This analysis reveals arguments over bills and parking spaces can be chalked up by police as crimes fuelled by hatred. At times this has boiled over into zeal, with police questioning members of the public for their opinions voiced online.

- The Government is fuelling a story about our country that is both not true, serves to do us down, and lower expectations. This is wrong.

- An appraisal of the best available evidence reveals acts of racial hostility, from violence to verbal abuse, to have declined substantially.

- Moreover, while the Government wants a decline in hate crime, the benchmark for measuring this against – the Crime Survey – is deeply flawed, with around half of race hate crimes being deemed to have a racial motive by survey respondents without a compelling reason. In essence, policy is shooting in the dark.

- At the same time, the Government is funding many organisations that have a vested interest in talking the problem up. These organisations offer for purchase improvements in other people's behaviour, which is a dubious tenet, while at the same time, seldom presenting a fair appraisal of the prevalence of the problem. This fuels misleading perceptions as well as generating forms of governance that are largely wasteful.

- Most damming of all, getting the numbers up has not resulted in a rise in prosecutions or convictions. Politicians have raised the expectations for justice only to fail to deliver.

- As a way forward, it is proposed that the Government legislates for the enhanced sentencing of crimes motivated by hatred where it is clearly evidenced that harm and culpability are greater.

- Proposals are made to reign in the vested interests, as well as enhance the way in which we measure hate crime statistically, to pave the way for a more honest appraisal of it.

Introduction

'All these hunters who are shrieking now
Oh do they speak for us?'
Leonard Cohen

There are no respectable political parties today, nor any with a real chance of gaining power in this country, that campaign on the wish to subjugate women to men, black and brown to white and so on. British people always tend, on the whole, to be revulsed by things such as Jim Crow segregation in the American South or Apartheid in South Africa.

Yet, we are convulsed with claims of inequality that rest largely on three sources. The first is individual incidents, but this is to risk the fallacy of composition – which is to make a judgement on the quality of the whole, based on an individual part of it. There are claims that the number of women murdered or black people shot dead by the police are not declining and that 'we are sick and tired of being sick and tired'. But as statisticians will tell you, such deaths are rare, and rare events conform to a different, constant and predictable pattern from common events. Simply put, in countries with large populations there will always be enough wicked individuals to do wicked things, and so you get a near-constant trickle of horror, assuming there are no major societal changes. But to correctly assess the progress

1

of women and ethnic minorities, you have to look at other indicators which show improvements, such as employment, educational attainment and earnings.

The second source of claims of inequality is statistical disparity between groups. I dealt with this idea in my last publication for Civitas, *How we think about disparity and what we get wrong*, so I will not repeat the ideas other than to stress that there are perfectly innocent statistical reasons why disparity exists between groups and it is impossible to infer discrimination from disparity where all things are not equal. Outcomes do not necessarily imply treatments.

The third is what is called 'hate crime', as it is reflected by hate crime statistics. Hate crime is the idea of crime motivated by hatred of the victim's group. Such statistics are important to political activists in that they can be presented as evidence of a particular group's 'oppression' at the hands of another.

The purpose of this report is to examine hate crime statistics in terms of what they show and their validity, as well as offering a critique of the ideas themselves that they reflect. But first consider the following extract from a recent article published in the *Daily Telegraph* by former-chief constable of Greater Manchester Police, Peter Fahy, in response to the death of Sarah Everard:

'The Stephen Lawrence report had a profound impact on policing during my 34-year career, and one of the crucial lessons was that the service to victims and families of victims has to be approached from their reality, emotions and perceptions, and not what an individual police officer or the police establishment think they should be.

'The statistics may say that young males are much more likely to be victims of violence and that a woman is far more likely to be attacked by someone known to her than by a stranger in the street, but this will not work to reassure women in the outpouring of experiences and emotions after the disappearance of Sarah Everard.'[1]

As I shall argue, the introduction of subjectivity into policing, or rather that police have a presumption of believing the victim exists behind so much of how we look at hate crime. Crimes are recorded as hate crimes and treated as such on the say-so of those reporting a crime. Evidence is only required in court. And while it is right that police should be respectful and courteous in their dealings with all members of the public, is it really true that we all have our own 'reality'? Are not the emotions and perceptions liable to mislead us?

As Macbeth asked, 'Art thou not, fatal vision, sensible to feelings as to sight?'

I take issue with Fahy's article in that he states that it is wrong to reassure people during contentious times with statistics that encourage a sense of perspective. While there are events that may shock us, they shock us because they are rare, and the evidence backs that up.

Moreover, Fahy has a double standard in that he requires the police not to quote reassuring statistics but is happy to refer to alarming statistical evidence himself:

'There have been so many surveys and studies showing that the day-to-day experience of so many women is one of harassment, unwanted sexual advance and aggression, in person and online, to the extent that it becomes their normality'.

It is wrong to allow alarmist claims to go unchecked since these have consequences. Believing you are likely to be sexually assaulted if you leave the house, or a victim of a racially-inspired attack if you venture out of your community, only serve to limit horizons. As we shall see, the fear of hate crime is much greater for ethnic minority people than its likelihood of occurrence. This may lead them to avoid certain places, and ultimately stymies community integration. A sense of perspective encourages a measured response. Hysteria encourages overreaction – and at what cost?

Since the European Union (EU) referendum, we have been inundated with stories of a 'rise in hate crime'. Such claims attract little scrutiny, but what basis do they have? As I show in Chapter 2, they rely on crimes recorded by the police. While the numbers are rising, the Office for National Statistics (ONS) specifically advises against their use as evidence of long-term trends, and the rise is attributed to better recording practices and greater reporting. Indeed, there is an entire cottage industry devoted to getting the numbers up. While there are spikes in recorded crime that are likely real, a spike by definition has both a rise and fall.

Moreover, the statistics from which genuine inference as to the prevalence of hate crime might be possible – the Crime Survey of England and Wales (CSEW) – show a decline. Such evidence tends to be downplayed in most official publications and is scarcely mentioned in the media, with pride of place given to the police figures. But as one criminologist put it to me, that the latter are invalid as evidence of a trend 'is what any first-year undergraduate learns'.

In this report, I examine the bulk of the available statistical evidence from the Crime Survey, police figures, and the Understanding Society surveys. My broad conclusion is that racially-inspired crime is declining, contrary to what is readily and widely believed. However, the numbers promulgated by the state are in themselves largely flawed, with many incidents being recorded that are neither crimes nor obviously motivated by prejudice, while the methodology behind the CSEW estimates relies on subjectivity and there is often no good reason for why survey respondents attribute a hate motivation to the crimes that befell them. In essence, policy is shooting in the dark.

But first, in Chapter 1, I undertake a review of the ideas behind hate crime and how they have been written into law. I find that the academic scholarship has no consensus as to what is meant by hate crime, but nevertheless, we have this taking ever-greater prominence in policy, law, and policing. The term 'hate crime' has no legal validity but is rather an umbrella term for a range of offences. Its existence in British law can be divided into that which regulates 'hate speech' and that which looks to punish with greater severity, crimes with a 'hate motivation'.

Law pertaining to hate speech began with attempts to stifle fascism in the 1930s, while there also existed a common law offence of sedition, defined as 'promoting hostility between different classes of His Majesty's subjects'. However, legislation has provided for further offences of stirring up of hatred, specifically to do with race, religion and sexuality. The liberal tradition was always for penalising speech that incited violence. An alternative version, which looked to enshrine in law the avoidance of offence, first pioneered by the Soviet bloc for entirely cynical reasons, is gaining greater foothold in our country.

Tougher sentencing for specific crimes, either as racially or religious aggravated, or in crimes where a hate motivation is established with reference to race, religion, sexuality, disability or transgenderism, was introduced by the last Labour government, starting with a manifesto commitment in 1997. The ensuing 1998 Crime and Disorder Act provided for specific racially aggravated crimes, all of which were already illegal in their basic form, only stiffer sentences were authorised. Nothing has been made illegal by hate crime legislation, only penalties have been increased.

The consequence of introducing protection on one strand of 'identity', namely race, was that it introduced inequality before the law, not between individuals, but between different characteristics. Muslim lobbyists complained they were not protected by racially aggravated offences as were Sikhs and Jews, and so the law was amended to include religiously aggravated offences.

The Law Commission is currently proposing that the number of protected characteristics be extended to include gender and age. The list is potentially endless, and there are no shortage of campaigning organisations that would gladly lobby for inclusion of their own favoured characteristics. Race begat religion, which begat sexuality, which begat disability, and so on and so on. Similar extensions are underway in Scotland, but surely time could be saved simply by seeking to punish generic hatred rather than having to name in law each and every strand. Does the Law Commission not realise this?

Moreover, it is arguable that the courts were already equipped to offer enhanced sentencing prior to 1998. What we are dealing with is an imbalance in the law, introduced by politicians seeking minority votes. We are now trying to correct this by introducing further imbalances when the obvious solution would be to remove the initial one.

Hate crime legislation offers steeper sentences for the same crimes, as distinguished by a motivation of hate. That such crimes are seldom motivated by hate, but rather thrill-seeking, while perpetrators might better be described as pitiful rather than hateful, are beside the point. If two crimes are the same, if sentencing must be proportionate to the offence, and the only thing that differentiates them is the motivation, then it follows that what is being punished is the thought itself. The Law Commission argues that motivation has always played a role in the law, which sees the *mens re*a, or guilty mind as in most cases, necessary to establish guilt. That is reasonable since it would be clearly wrong to punish someone for something done unintentionally. It is quite another, however, to make the *mens rea* an object of punishment.

The standard for the establishment of guilt is that *'The act is not culpable unless the mind is guilty.'* But what I argue is that we have ventured into a new way of doing law that inverts this, so that the mind is not guilty unless the act is culpable, and that we are punishing thought where it is seen as motivational. This is not hidden in the Law Commission's recent consultation document that states if ideas lead to crime, then the 'law rightly steps in'. But on what basis? The Law Commission's apologia for hate crime legislation offers argument by way of (thin) precedents, all the while oblivious to the truth that you cannot justify legal innovation through legal precedent.

Queen Elizabeth I of England famously said 'I have no desire to make windows into men's souls.' This was in reference to the provision of a common prayer book for her subjects, but no imposition of its interpretation upon them. It is taken as one of the cornerstones of liberalism 'that no government should intrude into the conscience of the citizen.'[2] But with hate crime legislation, have we not done this? Is this not to be objected to as an extension of government into thought and on a point of liberal principle?

A further problem with hate crime is that it creates a category of crimes that are not all immediately comparable in terms of their gravity. When I think of which crimes are the most serious, I prioritise those against body, then property, and then those against feelings last. It is wrong that someone might be frightened or abused in the streets by thugs as this imposes on their ability to enjoy life. But it should also be the case that human beings are expected to deal with each other, with the words they use, and to express favour or disfavour accordingly, and social sanctions if necessary. The point of law is to monopolise violence; the rest was always left to us.

But with hate crime, what you see are acts of violence classified together with acts of abuse, as relatively benign as name-calling. Government attempts to 'take hate crime seriously' have grown a cottage industry devoted to hate crime. While a small task force of hate crime workers exists to 'get the numbers up', what this results in practice is the police actively trawling for petty squabbles and ugly name-calling. This is at the expense of investigating crimes against body and property. As my analysis shows, what this results in is people reporting to the policy ugly arguments within their communities, sometimes even between friends and acquaintances.

The Government admits hate crime is declining, and sees this as evidence of the success of its strategy, but also claims that more needs to be done.

If something is falling, however, why do more? Policy, for the most part, amounts to spending money on various organisations that offer no services that might be successfully measured in terms of their success. Moreover, crime in general is on the decline, so it is hard to see how the Government's hate crime strategy is effective. And the organisations it encourages have every incentive to say things are bad and getting worse, but no incentive to ever say the reverse. A campaigning organisation that says everything is rosy does not last long. False claims of hate crime 'epidemics' only lower expectations and foster distrust and division, as well as poor decision making at the ballot box.

We are currently going through both an unprecedented restriction on liberty in response to a virus. On top of this, we have something called a 'culture war' – although such a term is misleading since this is nothing like what most soldiers would describe as a 'war'. Rather, what we have is what Neil Oliver has described as an 'attempted cultural revolution'. It is an attempt to re-write the cultural institutions of country. In order to do this, the new revolutionaries need convincing claims of the hostility of British life towards certain 'oppressed' groups. This is where hate crime fits in. If it can be shown that there is rising persecution, then it can be claimed that the culture is causal and can be rewritten or imposed anew.

But it is simply not true that hate crime is the norm, typical or rising, so far as the evidence will allow. The Government has largely kept itself out of this cultural dispute, preferring to remain aloof. This has been a mistake in that it has allowed it to fester to the point of attrition in the trenches of social media, with democratic disillusionment and exhaustion likely further steps. This is a Tory government with a hefty majority that could end this 'culture war' rapidly by putting its foot down.

Chapter 3 offers some modest proposals towards this endeavour. Among other things, I propose legislation that would, for the most part, repeal much of the existing legislation and restrict enhanced sentencing to generic hatred, where the crime in question is directed at intimidation of a specific group, as meted out against certain individuals within it. An example would be the attack on Muslims committed by Darren Osborne, or where a significant psychological harm can be evidenced. I further make proposals for reigning in the existing vested interests, including a code of conduct for the publication of statistics for organisations that receive government money and a prohibition on funding organisations that lobby for changes in the law.

Central to our approach should be to distinguish between harm and culpability. If more harm is genuinely evidenced then the penalty should be steeper. If an intention to do more than just hurt someone is genuinely evidenced, if an act of violence is intended as a signal to incite further violence, then the culpability is greater and thus, so too should be the punishment.

My intention is to provide, within the law, means for the adequate punishment of hate-fuelled crime, as well as lay the foundations for a more truthful appraisal of how we deal with hate crime. To be perfectly clear, I find intimidation and persecution abhorrent, as do most decent Britons. Crime motivated by hatred is something that can blight lives and in extreme cases, end them. But we cannot allow what is a noble sentiment behind the law to fuel useless governance, and what is ultimately further division and a narrative that only serves to do us down.

I would like to express my gratitude to Civitas for its support, as well as to those who read early drafts and provided comments.

1.

Hate crime: concept, law and politics

This chapter presents an overview of the ideas behind hate crime, their origin, the law, and their critique. It is argued that we have introduced some innovations into our law that stem from political interests and represent unchartered territory. We have moved into a new form of law where ideas are punished if they motivate crime rather than as necessary to establish guilt. This is a corruption of the traditional distinction between *mens rea* and *actus reus*. It can be objected to on principle alone.

This new form of law keeps growing in that we need more and more strands of characteristic-specific offences in order to placate advocacy groups that have a vested interest in 'hate'. The Macpherson report has been seminal in making matters worse by privileging subjective feeling over objective fact, which is against our legal tradition of how we deal with evidence, as well as fermenting an undue ideological influence on the police. This is part of what is termed 'woke' – but should be better understood as institutional capture – and is part of a wider trend in society that sees claims of victimhood as unquestionable. The gravity of the offence becomes enough to establish guilt, and the court of public opinion gradually has gained precedence over that of law or fact.

This is being fuelled by a government that wishes to be seen to be doing more to fight hate crime, despite the fact that by its own admission and contrary to popular understanding, it is falling.

Concept

We seldom appreciate that hate crime is a new idea in law. It trips off the tongue as though it has always been the case. That there are sceptics who question the suitability of such laws is not well known. The ideas behind hate crime are hard to pinpoint and critique since they both refer to something genuinely horrific in its most extreme manifestations but also, as I shall argue, change the law in a way that is radical.

The problem with new ideas is they tend to be invented, usually by intellectuals or academics who wish to propose something that is different to what went before – the old ideas. Typically, the assumption lying behind is that old ideas are a 'social construct', and therefore we can construct something new. However, such thinking can be criticised in the sense that old ideas may very well describe ways of thinking about and dealing with problems as they present themselves, while new ideas are often the imposition of social elites.

Moreover, the biggest problem with new ideas is that not everyone knows them, while even their proponents seldom agree as to what is meant. This can prove a recipe for misunderstanding and conflict.

Concerning hate crime, let us take two books, one hostile, the other supportive of hate crime laws – although not uncritical. In *Hate Crimes: Criminal Law & Identity Politics*, James B. Jacobs and Kimberly Potter argue for the repeal of hate crime legislation in the United States. Then take *Hate Crime: Impact, Causes & Responses* by Neil Chakraborti and

Jon Garland, who are supportive of hate crime legislation. Both pairs of authors are united in their highlighting of the vagueness behind the concept of hate crime.

As Jacobs and Potter make clear, the term 'hate crime' is new, while the phenomena it is hoped it will encapsulate is old. Human beings have been hurting each other based on their group characteristics since time immemorial. However, 'before the mid-1980s, the term "hate crime" did not exist'.

It is credited to the American legislators, John Conyers, Barbara Kenelly, and Mario Biaggi, all Democrats. Together they sponsored a bill in 1985, called the 'Hate Crime Statistics Act', that required the federal government to collect and promulgate statistics on crimes motivated by 'racial, religious, and ethnic prejudice'. Thereafter, usage of the term grew in the popular press – with more than one thousand articles on hate crime published in 1993, most diagnosing an 'epidemic'.[3]

Quoted in Jacobs and Potter is one sceptical article by John Leo:

'Most of the time it comes down to any... epithets hurled during the crime. This gets courts into a maelstrom... If a white mugs a black and delivers a slur in the process, is it a "hate crime" or an ordinary mugging with a gratuitous slur attached?'

In the 1990s, the term spread into legal scholarship.

In American law, hate crime refers to 'criminal conduct motivated by prejudice'. Jacobs and Potter question the validity of the concept in that it is not clear what is meant by 'prejudice', precisely which prejudices qualify, which crimes it might be applied to, and 'how strong the causal link must be between the perpetrator's prejudice and the perpetrator's criminal conflict'.

Where America leads, Britain follows, and so the concept of 'hate crime' made its way to these shores, although, as I shall argue, the actual body of law to which it is applied had begun some years prior.

Chakraborti and Garland provide an overview of the conceptual understanding of hate crime. The most striking thing about their explication is how little the emotion of 'hate' has to do with 'hate crime':

> '... the concept of hate crime is a harder task than might at first be imagined. We have seen the term "hate" is a problematic, ambiguous and in many cases inaccurate descriptor of the offences with which it is commonly associated...'

The second most striking thing is that so much of the academic discourse on what constitutes hate crime is wed to ideas of 'power-relations' between groups. Chakraborti and Garland both cite and distance themselves from an influential account by Barbara Perry, who views hate crime as about dominant groups keeping other groups in a state of submission; hate crime is an intended message to everyone, meted out on particular and unfortunate individuals. This is too restrictive in that it misses the point that so many individual victims of hate crime know their assailant, while Chakraborti and Garland found that 'in the majority of instances hate crimes are enacted for the excitement and thrill involved', with 'hate' not being the primary cause.[4]

A similar vagueness can be found in the Macpherson report and its explication of 'institutional racism'. Moreover, we see new ideas such as 'white privilege', plus structural, systemic, and symbolic racism. The acceptance of these is a sign of moral goodness, as well as matters of empirical fact. See for instance the (pointed) opprobrium reserved for the government advisor Munira Mirza for her comment that institutional racism was 'a perception more than a reality'.[5] And yet, not everyone knows to what is being referred.

The official definition of a hate crime is: 'Any crime that is motivated by hostility on the grounds of race, religion, sexual orientation, disability or transgender identity...'[6] However, in practice, the police use something slightly different, stressing subjective perception rather than objective fact, as laid out in the College of Policing's guidelines:

'A hate crime is any criminal offence which is perceived by the victim or any other person to be motivated by a hostility or prejudice based on:

- a person's race or perceived race, or any racial group or ethnic background including countries within the UK and Gypsy and Traveller groups
- a person's religion or perceived religion, or any religious group including those who have no faith
- a person's sexual orientation or perceived sexual orientation, or any person's sexual orientation
- a person's disability or perceived disability, or any disability including physical disability, learning disability and mental health or developmental disorders
- a person who is transgender or perceived to be transgender, including people who are transsexual, transgender, cross dressers and those who hold a Gender Recognition Certificate under the Gender Recognition Act 2004.'[7]

While a crime can be recorded as motivated by hostility, it must be evidenced as such in court. This begs the question of what is meant by 'hostility'. The definition, as used by the Crown Prosecution Service (CPS), is very wide and includes 'ill-will, spite, contempt, prejudice, unfriendliness, antagonism, resentment and dislike'. This is not defined in law.[8]

Somehow, it all does not add up. The police say a crime has been committed motivated by hostility. The crime goes to the courts where a jury then decides if a crime has been committed or not, and are asked to decide on whether or not it was fuelled by a forbidden motive. Are the police not overstepping their mark, in that it is up to the courts to decide if there has been a crime or not? As we shall see in the next chapter, police are recording unpleasant incidents as 'crimes' where the evidence for the motivation and the 'crime' are one and the same, namely offensive language. In fact, what you often see is an alternative motivation whereby people are arguing over something else – a space in the car park or a bill – and 'words are said'.

Surely the role of the police is to provide protection to individuals and their property and then collect evidence in order that a jury can say what happened. Is it lawful for the police or the government for that matter to say a crime has taken place, regardless of its motive?

Hate crime is a novel idea in law that breaks with our legal tradition in some crucial ways. The first relates to the distinction between *actus reus* and *mens rea*. Usually in law, a criminal offence both requires a criminal act – the *actus reus* – and criminal intention or a guilty mind – the *mens rea*.

The *mens rea* can include both 'malice aforethought', implying conscious planning or intent, or things less deliberate like negligence or recklessness. Some crimes require no proof of *mens rea* in order for a conviction to be secured under a condition of 'absolute liability'.[9] Hate crime radically extends what we have traditionally thought of as *mens rea* to include the group of the target of one's intention since 'hostility' would fall within the broad notion of 'malice aforethought'. There are implications to this. The standard common law test of criminal liability can be summed up as:

'The act is not culpable unless the mind is guilty.'

If hate crime is to be understood as punishing thought, which is a reasonable supposition since there are increased penalties for hate crimes relative to regular crimes, then it follows that we have created a whole new way of doing law whereby:

'The mind is not guilty unless the act is culpable.'

That is to say, you have a new legal order whereby thoughts are not to be punished unless they come into contact with a deed, in which case, they are fair game. I am not sure what the implications of this insight are, only to say that this change in our jurisprudence is not something to be entered into lightly. Moreover, one can object on a point of liberal principle that it is not for the state to punish thoughts, that thoughts do not make you do bad things but rather a lack of restraint – in short, a choice lies behind every wicked act.

A second implication is in what counts as evidence. In order to demonstrate hostility, prosecutors may look into the online communications or private affairs of the individual, such as postings on social media websites for instance. What matters in assessing guilt is not the scene of the crime, but the private and public utterances of the individual. Again, this is not something we should enter into lightly, since this is a significant expansion of the rights of the state into the sphere of individual liberty.

The third implication is that we radically reappraise how we prioritise both crime and punishment. Generally, the law has always prioritised the human body first, then property, with feelings given little protection. There is a proper role for the state to protect the feelings of the individual, in cases of menaces and threats. However, the novel creation of 'hate crime' has the effect of pulling all crimes against body, property, and feelings all into one category. Thus, prioritising hate crime, 'taking it seriously', overrides this basic hierarchy of the seriousness with which we naturally appraise crime. A slur becomes as serious as assault or arson.

The effect of this is you get police applying their limited resources to prioritise things that are both upsetting and trivial relative to other crimes. Being abused in the street or called racial slurs on social media do not compare to being assaulted, stabbed or sexually abused.

Creating such broad categories of crime that become politicised only serves to distort the priorities and incentives of the police and courts in fighting crime. It is time for the government to reassert the basic priorities of fighting crime and delivering justice. Merseyside Police recently got into trouble for a poster which erroneously claimed that 'being offensive is an offence'. This, as was pointed out by the Free Speech Union's Toby Young, is in ignorance of the law.[10] But what was not remarked upon was that the poster further claimed 'Merseyside Police stands with and supports the LGBTQI+ community, we will not tolerate Hate Crime on any level.'[11]

That is all very well, but there are such things as priorities. Is it really just to treat insults with zero-tolerance when resources are limited and some crimes are worse than others? Are the police not just fishing for reports they will likely be unable to do anything about?

It is hard to know what has gone wrong with the police, other than to say one suspects its operations have been taken over by a committed cadre of activists and campaigners who set the priorities but do not police the streets, taking in all the horrors of stabbings, murders, rapes and so on. One former police officer that I spoke to was clearly exasperated by the 'woke' takeover of the police – and he cannot be alone.

Moreover, the suspicion is that the police are only raising expectations over matters they are poorly placed to deal with. As seen in the graph below, in 2012/13, police in England and Wales recorded just over 20,000 crimes of racially or religiously aggravated public fear, alarm or distress, resulting in 7,500 charges and 1,200 cautions.[12]

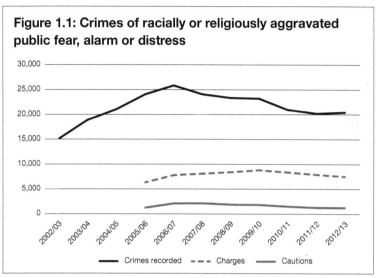

Figure 1.1: Crimes of racially or religiously aggravated public fear, alarm or distress

Source: Home Office, Ministry of Justice, and Office for National Statistics, 17 December 2013.

As well as the history of hate crime and speech legislation, laid out in the next section, it is important to consider the ideological conflicts that underwrote their development. An article published by the Hoover Institution, by Jacob Mchangama, called *'The Sordid Origin of Hate-Speech Laws'*, shows how the establishment of hate speech laws was influenced at international level, by the Soviet bloc of countries. He argues that the initial response of the West was to protect freedom of speech and that the instigation for this was all coming from Stalinist countries.

Given the general amorality of such regimes, it is hard not to believe that the whole purpose was to establish the right of the state to regulate speech in general and not just unpleasant speech. In fact, to regulate the unpleasant is by necessity to permit the pleasant, which is not the same thing as freedom.

Mchangama shows how the British tradition was always about looking to regulate speech that incited violence but not that caused offence. He further shows that one of the consequences of adopting the Soviet insistence on regulation of offensive speech has been that majority-Muslim countries have used the same language to justify suppression of religious mockery and satire – blasphemy and religious compulsion in other words.[13]

It is striking to think that in the absence of the Soviet Union we have come to agree with it. That Amnesty International can fail to afford Russian opposition leader Alexei Navalny its protection as a 'prisoner of conscience', meaning a political prisoner, because of 'hate speech' said years ago that has nothing to do with his current predicament, suggests this is getting out of hand and we have moved into a realm of extra-judicial regulation, where reputation is on trial and social media, rife with scarcely-hidden political interests, the jury.[14]

Law

While the term 'hate crime' is an American import, it has no basis in British law, but rather serves as an umbrella term for a body of law that has been developing since the 1930s. It would be accurate to describe the law as developing from general rules that sought to penalise incitement to violence between groups, to specific crimes for specific groups. This coincides with the rise of identity politics, which views society as divided into oppressed and dominant groups, with power a zero-sum game.

An authoritative account of the development of hate

crime law in the United Kingdom is given in the Law Commission's recent consultation paper, which provides the basis for what follows.[15]

The offence of inciting racial hatred was created in 1965 under the Race Relations Act. This was amended by the 1976 Race Relations Act to encompass the offence of 'stirring up racial hatred', whereby there was no longer need for any intention to foster hatred, albeit with safeguards remaining. This shift reflected a wider change in the law (section 8 of the Criminal Justice Act 1967) that 'abolished the presumption that person intends the natural and probable consequences of his act'.

The Public Order Act 1986 is the basis for much of our law on 'hate speech'. It updated the law so that speech or material must be threatening, abusive, or insulting, intended or likely to stir up hatred, and delivered either in public or private. There are, however, defences of a lack of intent as well as the so-called 'dwelling' defence, whereby the defendant had no expectation to believe what was said in a private dwelling was to be heard without. The offence of stirring up religious hatred was added in 2006, with that of stirring up hatred on grounds of sexuality subsequently added.

Hate crime law, beyond speech, begins with the 1998 Crime and Disorder Act, which introduced 'racially aggravated' versions of existing offences of assault, criminal damage, public order and harassment offences. These carry a longer maximum sentence than their 'mirror' offences. The same act also introduced 'enhanced sentencing' for all offences where the 'offender was motivated by or demonstrated hostility on the basis of race', in addition to the creation of the new aggravated offences. This was then consolidated into the wider enhanced sentencing provisions for all hate crime strands in subsequent legislation.

Hate crime law in the so-called devolved nations is broadly comparable, since much of the legislation predates devolution, although there are some differences. Reading the Law Commission's consultation, two issues are apparent but unaddressed. The first is the necessity of hate crime legislation, the second its continued development. The two are linked.

As the consultation makes clear, there was a common law offence of sedition which included 'promoting hostility between different classes of His Majesty's subjects'. In 1983, the Court of Appeal ruled that inciting racial hatred also fell foul of the common law 'because it amounts to sedition'. According to the Law Commission, it was 'only abolished' in 2009, as though such an offence was an embarrassing anachronism and not legally useful. Furthermore, the 1936 Public Order Act, which aimed at suppressing fascism, created an offence of 'offensive conduct conducive to breaches of the peace'.

And as the consultation makes clear, the courts had 'acknowledged racial motivation as an aggravating factor in sentencing' in 1994. Moreover, the courts are capable of adding new strands of hate crime themselves. In the 2007 case of the murder of Sophie Lancaster, the judge ruled that because the crime was motivated by her membership of 'goth' subculture:

> 'I regard this as a serious aggravating feature of this case, which is to be equated with other hate crime such as those where people of different races, religions, or sexual orientation are attacked because they are different... I add that the courts are perfectly capable of recognising and taking account of such aggravating features without the necessity of Parliament enacting legislation to instruct us to do so.'

His sentencing was upheld by the Court of Appeal, which ruled him 'fully justified'.[16]

The 1998 Crime and Disorder Act was introduced off the back of a 1997 Labour Party manifesto commitment to 'create a new offence of racial harassment and a new crime of racially motivated violence to protect ethnic minorities from intimidation'. The provisions were subsequently extended to religion because Sikhs and Jews were protected on ethnic grounds while other religions were not. Now, the purpose of the Law Commission's latest review is to see whether or not the law should be extended to other strands. All this begins because of politicians taking existing law and applying specific markers of identity to it, which only led to demands for more.

Manifesto commitments are made to win votes, and there is something cynical about Labour's 1997 commitment, in that ethnic minorities were already protected by the law because assault, for example, was already illegal irrespective of race. The thought seems to be that we need to appeal to ethnic minorities as victims of racism, and not just as individuals with a common interest in education, healthcare, law and order and so forth, just like everyone else.

Its effect was to introduce an imbalance in the law with subsequent, and at times wholly justifiable, claims from other groups, or specifically, advocacy groups, for protection based on other strands of identity. But all of these could of and can be dealt with by the courts and through the common law. Moreover, the problem with more and more facets of identity being added is that it detracts from the seriousness of the law and the esteem in which it is held. We might well agree that racist violence might be more harshly punished since this can spill over into intractable intracrine violence, but are we to expect the Goths to go to war with the Neds?

It should further be added that 'hate speech' laws are not restricted to just the 'stirring up' offences. The Crime and Disorder Act 1998 defined the offence of racially-aggravated harassment in part as a 'racially-aggravated course of conduct' – and conduct 'includes speech'. Harassment itself includes 'causing the person alarm or distress'.[17] Note also that the court case brought against footballer John Terry in 2012 for allegedly calling an opponent a 'black c***' was brought under the same act (Section 31(1)(c) – causing harassment, alarm or distress).[18]

Non-crime Hate Incidents
Matters are further complicated by 'non-crime hate incidents'. These are things that happen that do not amount to breeches of the law. The most recent College of Policing guidance on such incidents offers no explicit definition of what is a non-crime incident, other than to add that such a thing might be motivated by hostility in the same way as a crime. How do you define a negative other than to say it is everything the positive is not?

The guidance offers:

'Where it is established that a criminal offence has not taken place, but the victim or any other person perceives that the incident was motivated wholly or partially by hostility, it should be recorded and flagged as a non-crime hate incident.'

Records are taken which may show up on DBS background checks, largely at the police officer's discretion.

The collection of records of 'non-crimes' is justified on the grounds that it offers a monitorable picture of community relations, as well as the chance to intervene before matters escalate. It is also important to make records, given the natural ambiguity of social life, so police can later determine if a crime has or has not been committed, while actions that are not in themselves criminal might add up to a pattern of behaviour that is, such as stalking or harassment.[19]

Police reserve the right to intervene in such instances where no crime has been committed, but stress that their interventions must be proportionate. It is not immediately clear what the full arsenal of correctives they may issue are, although it seems from the guidance that they will offer a scolding, with victim support offered to those who claim victimhood.

There persists in the College of Policing guidelines ambiguity as to where the line lies between crime and non-crime. Consider the following illustrative example of a non-crime given:

'The victim reports that she was called a derogatory name referring to her disability, but the law has not been breached... Note: Name-calling or verbal abuse could amount to an offence under section 5 or section 4a of the Public Order Act 1986.'

Has the law been breached or has it not? Is this not an inevitable consequence of a lack of precise definition?

The Home Office does not publish statistics on hate incidents. Nevertheless, the *Daily Telegraph* has reported there have been more than 87,000 recorded in England and Wales over the last five years. It further reports that 'the number of criminal offences for which someone was charged or summonsed fell from 15.5 per cent to 7.8 per cent'.[20] Moreover, in 2018, 34,164 reports of crimes were abandoned, up 260 per cent on the year before, including 303 violent assaults resulting in injury.[21]

A freedom of information request made to the Metropolitan Police gives some illustration of what precisely is recorded.[22]

It formed the basis for a report in the *Daily Mail Online* which focused on some of the more ludicrous reports, including 'Suspect's dog barking at victim' and 'Informant feels his daughter was subjected to racial discrimination at a tennis match where line calls went against her'.[23]

The document itself reads as a litany of unpleasant interactions between human beings, which 20 years ago would have been regarded as part of life's rich tapestry but not a matter for the police. The typical incidents are people reporting slurs used in disagreements or people attributing particular forms of animus as lying behind them.

For example:

'Victim refused to take his shoes off at search and alleged racial profiling.' [Taking place at the airport.]

'Suspect has turned round and said something the victim finds racist.'

'Suspect has made racial comments to girlfriend whilst in a dwelling.'

It is also clear that many of the 'incidents' recorded may actually be crimes, without any ambiguity:

'VIW1 witness an unknown make kick a believed homeless female outside a supermarket causing her small pot of change to go over the pavement.' [Recorded as racial incident.]

Should the police really distinguish between crimes and incidents? Are not non-crime incidents a move into regulating behaviour where the police have no business? That is to say, unpleasant interactions that free individuals can deal with themselves through social sanctions or reconciliation and forgiveness.

Recently, the Home Secretary has sought to curtail the practice of recording such incidences, detailed in the section of this chapter on 'Developments'.[24]

Macpherson

It cannot be overstated how important the Macpherson report is to our story.

Not so long ago, the comedian Nish Kumar had an interesting exchange with the journalist Melanie Phillips on the BBC programme *Question Time* in discussion of stop and search.

'I'm furious with Melanie that she would sit in defence of stop and search, which is a racist policy, and that she would attack the Macpherson report and its attempt to drive institutional racism out of the police force. As I Londoner, I am incensed and disgusted by both of those responses. [sic]'

Stop and search is racist presumably, not because it is intended that ethnic minority people should experience it more, but because they do.

Phillips responded:

'Well, I am sorry that you are disgusted, but the fact is, I was disgusted by the Macpherson report, which I don't know whether you have read, have you?'

The reason this spat stuck in my mind was its use of the word 'disgust', and that criticising an official report might be deemed 'disgusting'. Judging by Kumar's response to Phillips, it was clear he had not read the Macpherson report, but nevertheless had held it in such high esteem, as to be disgusted by criticism of it.[25]

I suspect such sentiments are widely held, and it is hard to understand how this is possible. Indeed, it seems more reminiscent of a response to blasphemy than what we should expect in a civil society guided by reasoned debate where no position is regarded as having an automatic right to be respected or upheld. Note also, the howls of fury and disbelief that met Tony Sewell's Commission on Racial and

Ethnic Disparities when it found there was still racism in the United Kingdom but no evidence for institutional racism.

The Macpherson report, or to give it its proper name, the Report of the Stephen Lawrence Inquiry, was led by the late Sir William Macpherson and was published in 1999. Commissioned by Labour's Jack Straw, it examined the investigation by the Metropolitan Police into the murder of Stephen Lawrence in 1993. For the avoidance of any doubt, that crime was heinous, then and now. But because this is so, it does not follow that to criticise the Macpherson report is in some way a deviation from this position.

As well as detailing inadequacy in the Metropolitan Police's investigation, it was concluded to be 'institutionally racist'. However, the case for this is tendentious, while the concept itself is, as we shall see, a political and academic construct, subtle and easily misunderstood by the average person to mean 'riddled with racism' despite this never being the intention.

The Macpherson report saw a distinction between racism and 'institutional racism'. Its definitions were:

'"Racism" in general terms consists of conduct or words or practices which advantage or disadvantage people because of their colour, culture or ethnic origin. In its more subtle form it is as damaging as in its overt form'.

'"Institutional racism" consists of the collective failure of an organisation to provide an appropriate and professional service to people because of their colour, culture or ethnic origin. It can be seen or detected in processes, attitudes and behaviour which amount to discrimination through unwitting prejudice, ignorance, thoughtlessness, and racist stereotyping which disadvantage minority ethnic people.'

However, the concept of institutional racism is nebulous, with many different definitions offered, as is made clear by the Macpherson report. It details the concept's history with its origins among the Black Panthers, as well as competing definitions of it supplied to the inquiry by academics and organisations, such as the now defunct Commission on Racial Equality. It is a subtle concept, easily misconstrued and hard to grasp, but in effect amounts to racist outcomes without necessarily racist actors. Attributing a motivation (racism) to an outcome is, however, a logical absurdity. How can the same signifier be applied to two completely different 'signifieds'?

Moreover, the perfectly reasonable concern of the then Metropolitan Police commissioner, Sir Paul Condon, that such conceptual niceties would be easily mistaken for evidence of a police force full to the rafters with racists and that this would be damaging to moral and trust, were swept aside.

The Macpherson report gives a short summary of where it found institutional racism which can be summarised as:

a) The manner of the investigation, including how the Lawrence family and witnesses were treated and the failure of 'many officers to recognise Stephen's murder as purely "racially motivated" crime';

b) Disparity in stop and search which, despite all the other variables which may account for it, 'there remains, in our judgement, a clear core conclusion of racist stereotyping';

c) Under-reporting of 'racial incidents' which is due to a lack of trust, which despite other possible explanations, 'we find irresistible the conclusion that a core cause of under-reporting is the inadequate response of the Police Service'; and

d) A lack of adequate training evidenced by 'a single officer questioned before us in 1998 [having] received any training of significance in racism awareness and race relations throughout the course of his or her career.'

The Macpherson Report did not conclude that the majority of police officers were motivated by racist sentiment, nor did it find any evidence of racist language, other than the usage of terms such as 'negro' and 'coloured'. Such terms have not always been as offensive in the past as they are today.[26] Nor was it concluded that policing policy was racist in intent. As was stated in Macpherson:

'In this Inquiry we have not heard evidence of overt racism or discrimination'.[27]

Instead, we have a claim to truth based on the four empirical pieces of evidence listed above.

These can be disputed on reasonable terms. Regarding (a), there is no comparator given by Macpherson, that is to say, no evidence that a murder investigation involving a white victim might have been better conducted; (b) a study conducted by the Home Office (2000 – near-contemporaneously with the Macpherson report) found disproportionality in stop and search could largely be accounted for by people of an ethnic minority being more likely to be available to be stopped and searched;[28] (c) there are many other types of crime or incident that go underreported for reasons such as it being unlikely the police will be able to do anything about it; and (d) much of the training described is largely ineffective in changing behaviour – but the extent to which this is meaningful evidence is hard to gauge.

Then consider the following from David Green on the police's investigation into the murder of a white woman:

'At almost the same time that Stephen Lawrence was killed, Rachel Nickell was murdered on Wimbledon Common. The police made a hash of that investigation too, making even greater blunders than in the Lawrence case. The police did at least identify the murderers of Stephen Lawrence but were unable to make charges stick. In the Nickell case they wasted years pursuing the wrong person. If there was a systemic problem at the time, it was poor quality police investigation, not racism.'[29]

The Macpherson report has wider implications in our story of the development of hate crime. Recording of racially-motivated incidents above and beyond racist criminal activity was instigated as the Macpherson inquiry was ongoing. The creation of the Racial and Violent Crime Task Force (RVCTF), led by John Grieve in 1998, was based at the London Metropolitan Police. This was an initiative created by the commissioner at the time, Sir Paul Condon. The RVCTF was set up, in part, to track known racist criminals. It was decided that all race-related incidents would be recorded to monitor community tension, above and beyond reports of racist criminal activity. Today, Grieve sits on the government's independent advisory committee on hate crime.

But it is Macpherson's insistence on under-reporting of racist crime as evidence of 'institutional racism' which we have come to consider under the hate crime umbrella, which is central to our story since this is the source of official efforts to increase the number of recorded incidents.

Perhaps though, the unintended consequence of Macpherson is that in damning the Met and the police in general by extension, what is called a 'purity spiral' was created – whereby the police could never fully demonstrate how it might become no longer institutionally racist, especially since so much of the charge hinges on disproportionality in stop and search. To deny the charge was evidence of it.

Senior police officers could never quite be good enough, and so we have seen insults on social media websites and questionable or unfashionable views treated as worthy of police attention at the same time as crimes such as burglary are downgraded. Moreover, in recommending community involvement in policing, it has not improved accountability but opened the door for unaccountable activists to lobby the police through so-called Independent Advisory Groups (IAGs).

The Macpherson report is also the source of the victim's subjectivity in defining what is or is not a racist incident. It recommended: 'A racist incident is any incident which is perceived to be racist by the victim or any other person'.[30]

This was not the invention of subjectivity; prior, the definition used since 1985 had been at the police officer's discretion.[31] What it meant was that the public could define how the police classified incidents. Moreover, Macpherson stipulated that both crimes and non-crimes should be recorded by the police, as well as making provisions for third-party reporting. Present also is the idea, resurfacing lately in both the Law Commission's consultation and the recent Scottish Hate Crime Bill, that racist language used in private should be prosecuted. The law might very well govern public order, but private too?

Perhaps though the greatest harm has been that Macpherson made it harder for the police to offer protection in crimes such as 'honour' abuse, sexual exploitation, knife crime and so on, whereby there is disproportionate ethnic minority involvement. This is through making it too difficult to talk about race, as well as disproportionate police attention being evidence of institutional racism. The result is that the police fail to offer an appropriate service to, among others, members of an ethnic minority, and so the charge of institutional racism is sufficient to bring it about. But a point widely missed by those supportive of Macpherson is that if reports are going up, institutional racism must be in retreat, given the terms of that inquiry.

Developments

There are four major developments to hate crime policy and legislation in the works. The first is the Law Commission's proposals for reform:

- Establish criteria for deciding whether or not additional characteristics should be included in hate crime legislation.

- Add sex/gender to the list of 'protected characteristics'.

- Create aggravated and stirring up offences for all strands.

- Create aggravated versions of offences contained in legislation pertaining to malicious communications.

It has considered and consulted publicly on the following:

- Increasing the application of enhanced sentencing.

- Make it easier to prosecute crimes against the disabled.

- Create a 'Hate Crime Commissioner' to 'drive forward best practice in preventing hate crime and supporting its victims'.

- Bring together all hate crime legislation into one 'Hate Crime Act'.[32]

It has been reported that the Commission has rowed back on its plans to remove the 'dwelling defence' for stirring up hatred.[33] It has further consulted on whether or not to include such characteristics as: age, sex workers, homelessness, alternative subcultures, and philosophical beliefs.

The chief failing of the Law Commission is its inability to

perceive correctly what it is doing. As its own consultation document shows, the law was capable of prosecuting hate crime prior to the advent of characteristic-specific provisions, either in terms of the law on sedition or through treating hatred as an aggravated factor in sentencing. What we had was law that applied to all and protected everyone.

The Law Commission's failing is to not perceive that it is proposing correctives to past political meddling in the law.

The second major development is the passing in March of this year of the Scottish government's Hate Crime and Public Order Act. This accomplishes a number of things. Firstly, it repeals those sections of the Crime and Disorder Act 1998 that create racially aggravated offences. Instead, the act allows for treating any offence as aggravated where a motive of prejudice, pertaining to age, disability, religion, sexual orientation, transgender identity or race/ethnicity is evidenced. Secondly, it extends the existing offence of stirring up hatred to encompass all such characteristics.

The act was spearheaded by Scotland's justice secretary, Humza Yousaf. On its passing he declared: 'I truly believe the period of Parliamentary scrutiny the Bill has undergone has shown Holyrood at its very best – a collaborative, diverse and determined Parliament which we should all be proud of.'

This though is disingenuous in that he is presenting what was actually a considerable rebuke to him as somehow a victory. The act passed has been criticised as illiberal by the Institute of Economic Affairs' Marc Glendening, among others, but in truth it is mild in comparison to the initial bill. That can rightly be described as draconian and appalling.[34] For instance, it looked to make illegal the possession of 'inflammatory material', as well as behaviour that would supposedly stir up hatred based on 'likelihood' rather than intent.[35] All this was stripped from the act itself, with a 'reasonable person' test added, as well as a beefed-up section on freedom of speech.[36] But the bill itself betrays a political imagination that offers Braveheart but without the freedom.

The act has drawn renewed criticism in that it offers no 'dwelling defence', meaning it criminalises private utterances. Former SNP politician Jim Sillars said:

'The new legislation is going to open up lots of people – who do not intend to direct hate at anyone – to find themselves being reported to the police for hate crimes.

'And there will be lots of malicious and vexatious complaints because most people are not lawyers and will tend to define hate crime as they see it, and not necessarily as the law sees it.

'And so the definitions that Humza Yousaf has insisted on putting into this bill will be tested in the forensic forum of a court, and I believe that's when, suddenly, all will be revealed about its flaws.'[37]

The criticism is that for all the intent that has gone into defining what is a hate crime, what are protected characteristics, and what is legitimate or not, this will not match with how real people respond to the legislation or how it applies to them in actuality. Will this not just lead to family members reporting each other? Will the provision made for free speech be adequate?

Overlooked in the discussion of the act has been the introduction of clauses that mandate the Scottish government to publish statistics pertaining to the number of convictions as well as crimes recorded by the police. These provisions were not present in the initial bill.

There are no good numbers on hate crime in Scotland; what you get are the numbers of crimes passed on by the police for prosecution. These are insufficient to evidence the actual prevalence. But the act itself blunders in that it commands the Scottish government to produce statistics that will likely fuel misconceptions, in that police numbers will show rises which will be interpreted (often deliberately) as increasing prevalence. This is thus a boon to the hate crime industry. Any future publication on behalf of the Scottish government must include evidence from the Scottish Crime Survey.

The act adds age as a protected characteristic while provision for the future addition of sex is made. Whether or not this is done will be at the discretion of Baroness Helena Kennedy – who will make a recommendation on the matter after further inquiry.[38] She will be paid £1,000 per day, working two to three days a week for up to 12 months. That means she will be paid, at most, £36,000 of taxpayers' money, while others working on her inquiry get nothing other than their expenses met.[39]

Mr Yousaf has proven himself capable of deciding that age should be a protected characteristic, but does not see himself capable, as a democratically elected politician, to decide on the inclusion of sex. He has consulted women's organisations that, as minutes of his consultations show, have presented him with arguments for and against, yet still feels the need to get someone who is unelected to make the decision for him, and at considerable expense.[40]

The third substantial development is the government's recent announcement that the police will record misogyny as a hate crime, made shortly after the death of Sarah Everard. This is supposedly on an 'experimental basis', but smacks of a panicked response out of the wish to be seen to do something. Moreover, it may be interpreted as strong-arming the Law Commission into conclusions by creating 'facts on the ground'. It is also reported in the *Daily Mail Online* that this is a 'concession to campaigners'; that is to say, acquiescing to something long-demanded in a moment when passions are running high and the likelihood of objection low. Fawcett Society chief executive Felicia Willow called it a 'major step forward in changing how we understand, address and prevent violence against women – and one that we hope will change attitudes towards women'.[41]

But what precisely is meant by misogyny? How will attaching this label add anything to how we count the number of crimes such as rape or sexual assault, or understand why people do such things? Why do we not already know this after decades of feminist-led criminology? Moreover, are such crimes really motivated by hatred of women? If a man rapes a woman, is he a misogynist motivated by hatred of women, or is he motivated by a desire to have sex? If he rapes a man, is he a misandrist and do we need to record misandry as a hate crime too? Is assuming a motivation really beneficial to crime prevention? Surely it would be best just to have a mass campaign telling people such things are deeply wrong.

Moreover, it should be pointed out that the Fawcett Society has an interest in having the category of 'hate crime' attached to crimes committed against women since it adds gravity to their campaigns, as well as providing a source of official statistics which encompass a wide range of crimes, sufficient to produce a large number. The bigger the number, the bigger the profile.

Fourthly, the Home Secretary, Priti Patel, has written to the College of Policing, asking it to review its practice of recording non-crime hate incidents, in particular where individuals are named and this shows up in background checks.[42]

Policy

Current government policy on hate crimes is outlined in a document called 'Action Against Hate: The UK Government's plan for tackling hate crime – two years on', published in 2018. It rests on five key planks:

1) Prevention to 'challenge harmful narratives before they develop into hatred' by:
   a) Funding campaigners, including the Anne Frank Trust;
   b) Supporting the education sector in 'educating and protecting' young people from hate; and
   c) Challenging prejudice in wider society, including the media[!].

2) Response.
   a) An online harms white paper;
   b) 'Particular support' to vulnerable communities; and
   c) Improving training for police and others to better respond to hate crime.

3) Increasing reporting.
   a) Improving reporting and recording...; and
   b) Specifically with regard to disability.

4) Improve support for victims.
   a) A Law Commission review into the adequacy of the law (currently ongoing);
   b) Improved support; and
   c) 'Supporting specific communities who are particularly vulnerable'.

5) Increasing understanding through:
   a) Engaging with specific communities...;
   b) Expert groups; and
   c) 'sharing experiences and expertise'.

The underlying assumption is that reductions in crime can be brought about by government both bettering law and practice, and purchasing knowledge and improvements in the behaviour of other people from third parties.

There are some good things here, some that are toothless but sound good, and also the concern that this is simply good for vested interests in order to better address a problem which the same document argues is declining in its prevalence. While money provided for additional security measures for places of worship or cultural significance are in principle a good thing, we seldom find out how they are spent.

Ultimately, the problem is that hate crime has become a matter of being seen to be virtuous, and so politicians throw money at it. Those who get the money have no incentive to say things are getting better, because that will mean less money. The government is happy to claim a fall in hate crime recorded by the Crime Survey as evidence of its success, but that 'there is more to do' because the number of victims remains 'too high'. However, the same survey shows crime in general to be falling, so government strategy cannot be pinpointed as causal in the decline of hate crime. But instead of simply giving it more time, the government commits to more action. In the real world we say 'if it ain't broke, don't fix it'. In government, we say 'if something is being mended, mend it some more'.

My Civitas colleague Joanna Williams has written about what she calls 'hate crime entrepreneurs' dedicated to a particular social group that have a strong vested interest in both higher numbers of hate crimes and government funding for initiatives to tackle the problem. The two are linked in that the greater the problem, the bigger the budget. They also campaign for 'ever looser definitions of hate crime and ever more expansive cohorts of victims'. Since they are often in receipt of government money, they are 'effectively paid by the government to tell government ministers (via civil servants) what they want to hear'.

Organisations listed in the updated action plan include the Anne Frank Trust, Kick It Out, Show Racism the Red Card, Tell MAMA and Galop, among others. The Ministry of Housing, Communities and Local Government runs a grant scheme for organisations concerned with 'faith, race and hate crime'. In 2020/21 it gave out £1.8 million in grants to, among others, the English Football League (£287,740), the Antony Walker Foundation and Agent Academy (£269,201), the New Vic Theatre (£222,931), and the Newcastle United Foundation (£120,029).

The government aims to back projects that 'champion the government's commitment to building a diverse and tolerant society for all faiths and races' that provide 'school workshops, peer education and in school ambassadors'. While this work may be beneficial, we had such workshops at my school and the kids I would rate as most likely to commit a hate crime paid them no heed. Moreover, why the government is backing the charitable arm of a Premier League football club is anyone's guess.

Another pot of money is put aside for security upgrades to places of worship or of cultural significance. The current amount allocated is £3.2 million as of June 2020. When the scheme was first announced, it stood at £800,000 per year, doubled to £1.6 million in 2019.[43] On top of this, a £5 million pot was announced over three years for a 'training programme'.[44] In addition, the Community Security Trust receives £14 million from the government each year to provide security for Jewish sites. However, the evidence would suggest that much of the general pot of money is not taken up. A freedom of information request revealed the following monies were allocated in the last five years:

Table 1.1: Home Office funding awarded under the Places of Worship Protective Security Scheme	
Year	Funding
2016/17	£435,466.65
2017/18	£440,203.38
2018/19	£806,281.92
2019/20	£1,718,765.72
2020/21	£1,704,237.46

Source: Home Office FOI

Government policy has further been to back 'third-party reporting'. This is the practice of organisations that provide resources for the reporting of hate crime. The idea is that people from minority groups either do not trust the police or feel uncomfortable going to them, so it is good to have a third-party to help facilitate things.

There exists a myriad of organisations offering third-party reporting, some more professional than others. The largest, what might be termed 'big third-party reporting', are Galop ('LGBT'), the Community Security Trust (CST) (Jewish), and Tell MAMA (Muslim).

The Government's plan to tackle hate crime commits it to supporting an increase in third-party reporting where it is believed underreporting is occurring, as well as identifying more locations, both in the public sector and outside, where reporting can be done.

However, some scepticism about third-party reporting organisations was expressed in a review by the National Policing Hate Crime Group – which concluded that many 'failed to deliver tangible results' or had short lifespans.[45] This is further backed up by a review of third-party reporting centres conducted by the Barnet Safer Communities Partnership Board. It found that those organisations operating in Barnet displayed 'little activity' – with the exception of the CST and Galop. Most third-party reporting sites did not advertise their role and had offered no training to staff. It concluded: 'Staff take very few reports and complain that when they do there is no feedback mechanism to let them know what has been done with the report'.[46]

It would also appear that third-party reporting does very little in terms of actually gathering reports of hate crime to be sent to the police. Data from the Metropolitan Police show that between January and October 2016, of the 14,123 religious or racially motivated hate crimes that were reported, just 47 came from third-party reporting centres. Contrast this with 10,927 coming from a simple call to the police (with 300 coming from the internet or through email). Out of 1,031 reports of Islamophobic hate crime in this period, just 10 came from third-party reporting, while for anti-Semitic reports there were just two out of 413. (This raises the question of where Tell MAMA and CST reports are going – it is possible that the Metropolitan Police is not adequately recording the sources of hate crime reporting).[47]

The suspicion that third-party reporting does very little to bring in reports of hate crime is further confirmed by an audit of an unnamed police force. The audit published by the Office for Criminal Justice Reform – focused on the first 95 reports of hate crimes made after October 2007. Just two per cent of cases were reported via a third-party centre.

There is also little evidence of a coherent approach to third-party hate crime reporting. A survey of hate crime third-party reporting organisations conducted by the Home Office found that of those who responded, just one half used the official working definition of hate crime. Moreover, it is not immediately evident that third-party reporting is any more accessible than calling 999. Of the 113 organisations that responded to the survey, 46 admitted not being able to take reports by phone, while 39 could not take them in person.

The argument for third-party reporting is that they offer familiarity and comfort to victims, often from 'marginalised' communities. However, the Home Office survey found that out of 113 organisations responding to the survey, 81 offered no advocacy services, while 105 offered no translation services. Thirty-one organisations admitted to not providing any specialist support to victims reporting hate crimes. Ten even admitted to not passing on reports to the police.

To top things off, it may very well be the case that the police report more hate crimes to the third-party reporting organisations than the other way around. There exists, between the police and the big third-party reporting organisations, data sharing agreements that allow the police to share information on crimes and incidents with Tell MAMA, the CST, Galop and Stop Hate UK.[48] For example the agreement for Tell MAMA reads that its purpose is:

'To provide Tell MAMA with up-to-date information relating to incidents which involve members of the Muslim community. This will better prepare Tell MAMA to protect the Muslim and other sections of our community and to provide advice which will help citizens to protect themselves and their communities.'[49]

All of these organisations receive public funding.[50] What we have is in effect the taxpayer paying the police to report crime to organisations that he is also paying to report crime to the police. Moreover, what advice could Tell MAMA give to victims of hate crime that could not be given by the police?[51]

Reporting of hate crimes is remarkably easy, but then it is easy to report any crime. All you have to do is call 999. But in addition to this basic service, there are apps and websites, with one in particular standing out – True Vision. This website is run by the National Police Chief's Council and allows for the (anonymous) reporting of crimes, incidents and 'online hate material'.[52]

Advising the government on hate crime is the Independent Advisory Group on Hate Crime, which sits within the Home Office. Details of who sits on this group are not immediately forthcoming on the government website, but a freedom of information request revealed it is made up of mostly academics and advocacy groups. Below are the names of the members of the group and the organisations they represent, as of March 2021:

- Mike Ainsworth – Independent Chair of the Group;

- Iqbal Bhana – Deputy Chair of the Group and represents race groups;

- Professor John Grieve – Former Deputy Assistant Commissioner in the Metropolitan Police;

- Leni Morris – CEO Galop, London's LGBT community safety charity;

- Josh Bradlow – Stonewall, and represents LGB interests;

- Dr Nathan Hall – Senior lecturer in criminology and policing at the Institute of Criminal Justice Studies at the University of Portsmouth;

- Jemma Tyson – Academic at Portsmouth University and chair of the Youth IAG;

- Sylvia Lancaster – Founded the Sophie Lancaster Foundation and represents 'alternative subcultures' interests;

- Yasmin Rehman – Advocate for human rights, with specific expertise around attacks on women and people who leave religions;

- Professor Sue Sanders – Co-Chair of 'Schools Out', a voluntary organisation supporting LGBT teachers and drivers of LGBT History Month;

- Dr Robina Shah – Psychologist and academic researcher by profession, and the National Lead for Disability Hate Crime for the Department of Health and Ministry of Justice;

- Mike Smith – Former Commissioner in the Equality and Human Rights Commission (EHRC);

- Mike Whine – Director of Government and International Affairs with the Community Security Trust (CST);

- Emma Nuttall – Director of Friends, Families and Travellers (FFT), and represents gypsy and traveller communities' interests on the Group;

- Fiyaz Mughal – Director, Faith Matters;

- Iman Atta – Tell MAMA;

- John Azah – Director, Kingston Race Equalities Council.

A precursory glance at some of these names' online presence reveals them, for the most part, to be reasonable people, although some are obviously promoting identity politics. The more pressing question is the extent to which they are truly independent. For instance, the same freedom of information request revealed that in the past five years, the

Home Office has funded Galop by £29,000 for 'projects in the first round of the Hate Crime Community Projects Fund', as well as £1,221,375 since 2016/17 for a 'helpline, some specific projects and additional support during the Covid-19 pandemic to support LGBT+ victims of domestic abuse'.

If you are advising government on a policy area from which your organisation derives substantial amounts of government funding, you are not independent and have a substantial conflict of interest. Representatives of Tell MAMA, the CST, and related organisations, are also in this bind.

Reading the organisations represented, you are left with the impression of many people who would say 'yes, yes, and yes', but few who would say 'really?' Note how policy on the matter which promises more reporting, more research and more 'community engagement' fits the interests of such groups well. But this aside, it is not entirely clear what this independent advisory group does or what advice it provides, since no details are published. While it is proper that government solicits knowledge from external sources, is it really necessary that it embeds external experts within?

Enthusiasm
There are notable examples where the police have overstepped the mark. For instance, the political commentator and activist Darren Grimes and the historian David Starkey faced prosecution for an interview broadcast online, in which the latter put forward the proposition that the transatlantic slave trade could not have been a genocide because 'there wouldn't be so many damn blacks in Africa or in Britain, would there?'

As Dr Starkey has admitted, his words were offensive, but clumsily used to convey the idea that there were many black people in the world today. That this is an argument against the idea that the transatlantic slave trade qualifies as 'a genocide' is both fallacious and beside the point.

In his interview, Dr Starkey was withering in his criticism of the police itself, as well as political, cultural and academic orthodoxy. As he said: 'Has there been anything more shocking than policemen going down on their knees before rioters? What is the symbolism of that?'

Mr Grimes also criticised the police for selectively applying the law regarding Black Lives Matter (BLM) protests. It was difficult not to infer that the police were shaking down their critics.

Then you have the case of the inimitable Harry Miller, a former police-officer and businessman who, in response to satirical content posted online, received a call from police. Mr Miller recounted the exchange thus:

'PC Gul described it as a limerick. It wasn't, but that is beside the point. My retweeting of a gender critical verse had apparently so enraged someone from 'down South' that they felt it their civil duty to act as Offended-in-Chief on behalf of my employees 'up North.' Not that anyone from my firm of around 90 staff had complained, of course, but again... that's beside the point. PC Gul rang my work, spoke to my MD, then spent 32 minutes lecturing me on hurt feelings and in-vitro body parts accidentally growing from a lady brain as I sat with my shopping at Tesco. Sarcasm, satire and talk of synthetic breasts was sufficient to prompt the most urgent of police intervention. That PC Gul didn't appear in Tesco car park with his blues and twos blaring, I suppose, is a small mercy.'

'Were any of the tweets criminal?' I ask.

'No,' says PC Gul.

'Then why are you ringing me?'

'I need to check your thinking,' says PC Gul.

A police spokesman later told the police: 'We take all reports of hate incidents seriously and will always investigate and take proportionate action.'

There are other examples of police intervention in what are, to the untrained eye, simply utterances made online that offend those who are highly sensitive as well as politically active, such as the cases of Graham Linehan and Posie Parker.[53]

This is shocking and can be traced back to the creation of the 'non-crime incident', as well as official directives of zero-tolerance. Non-crimes can receive non-punishments, in terms of reputational damage. A police visit to your work is sufficient to lower your reputation within the community, this incidentally being the legal test for libel. That Mr Miller has a 'hate incident' against his name, without any substantiation or verification and based solely on someone else's objections, might be tantamount to having a shadow criminal record.

Does he not deserve, at the very least, a non-trial?

There is a concern that the police have been subjected to an ideological takeover by campaigning organisations that both push the idea of hate crime as a problem that is getting out of hand, and ideological concerns that are contentious and far from settled. For instance, each year police forces pay thousands of pounds to Stonewall.[54] Stonewall audits the police as to whether it is friendly towards gay and transexual people. The effect of this is to establish Stonewall's position as arbitrator of what is good and bad within the police. This is not a neutral body in the same way that the official inspectorate of the police is.

In addition to the purchasing of indulgences from such groups, police may come under the sway of identarian activists through Independent Advisory Groups. These are panels of members of the community who advise the police. They were established off the back of the Macpherson report which 'recommended the involvement of local people in policing'. According to past College of Policing guidance, 'the role of an IAG is to help us to build insight into the needs, wants and assets of the groups who are under-represented in our normal decision-making processes'.[55]

Thames Valley police describes its groups as having 'Membership [which] seeks to be reflective of the protective characteristics held within the Equality Act 2010'. Thus, the terms of reference encourage the seeking out of identity group advocates rather than prominent and trusted figures in the community, comparable to school governors. While its minutes are published, contributions from the Thames Valley IAG members are anonymous. The same police force states 'IAGs consider local issues such as stop and search figures, hate crime statistics, critical incidents or issues raised as relevant and topical to the public that the LPA serve'.[56]

Perusing the minutes of these organisations reveals the concerns of various advocacy groups to be at the forefront. Minutes from a Thames Valley IAG meeting in 2020 show that police were actively looking to recruit from the Black Lives Matter movement:

'The Local Police Commanders have been tasked to increase representation, particularly on the back of Black Lives Matter Movement, to make sure they are reaching out to organisers of protests – High Wycombe has been successful- they have 4 x new members coming into their IAG.'[57]

Recall that, under the lockdown rules at the time, such protests were illegal, while BLM has a radical core that is hostile to the police.[58]

Hate crime pops up frequently within such documentation. For instance, minutes from a Norfolk Police independent advisory group state:

'The Norfolk IAG has continued to act as a critical friend to Norfolk Constabulary, particularly focusing on hate crime throughout the year. Some members have undertaken research to gain a better understanding of the experiences of the LGBTQI+ community in relation to homophobia and hate crime incidents. The members are working with Norfolk constabulary to analyse the research and look at better ways to engage with the LGBTQI+ community moving into 2021.'

And:

'A Transgendered Volunteered Support Worker from the Norfolk LGBT Project thanked members of IAG for the invitation to the AGM. The support worker observed that there has been no direct engagement from the police with regards to the Transgendered community in recent times. The support worker went on to ask if there was any specific hate crime data related to LGBT hate crime.

'Brian Walker (IAG member) introduced himself and explained that as a member of the LGBT community, he too has an interest with regards to LGBT hate crime data. BW explained that in his role as an IAG member, he is currently scrutinising data produced by the constabulary and is conducting a piece of research with another IAG member and the OPCCN. BW explained that the research is focusing on LGBT hate crime and examining if such incidents are been reported by those who experiences of this crime. [sic]'[59]

This shows the possibility for which advocacy groups can have privileged access to the police in a manner that is not always transparent, and how they can use it to push hate crime up the agenda. Such schemes are set up to increase transparency and engender trust, but it is doubtable that any of the disaffected in society have ever heard of any of the individuals involved or the work they do. It is time for a full and proper inquiry by Her Majesty's Inspectorate of Constabulary and Fire & Rescue Services (HMICFRS) into precisely how these groups are put together, scrutinised and draw funding out of the police. Government should seek democratic alternatives, such as regular town hall meetings.

One senior police officer with responsibility for hate crime told me 'every community wants to talk about hate crime' and that 'if it matters to the community, then it matters to us'. Yet, polling by Policy Exchange of British Muslims has shown Islamophobia to be rather low on their list of concerns. Only six to seven per cent say harassment on grounds of religion or ethnicity is a big problem.[60] The Law Commission speaks of what groups want, but, in reality, they are referring to what unrepresentative, unelected lobbyists say they want. The same Policy Exchange polling found the Muslim Council of Britain enjoyed the support of between two and four per cent of British Muslims, with most of that London-based.

Campaigners have begun to target children. West Oxfordshire Community Safety Partnership is a coalition of 'Thames Valley Police, Oxfordshire County Council, voluntary and community sector groups, and housing organisations'. It recently ran a competition in local schools for children to 'create a piece of work that would both inspire and educate'. The competition winner, an 11-year-old girl, is quoted in the *Witney Gazette* as saying:

'I have noticed a lot of young people are being targeted and it is all about talking to them. At the same time, a lot of people are not aware of what is going on in people's lives. It could be really affecting them and causing them to have bad thoughts'.

She produced a poster with the slogan 'Stop the Hate' – which urged people to report racism and homophobia to the police. The runner up made a poster about Black Lives Matter.[61]

Children of that age are too young to engage in such matters. They only mean well, and this initiative is purely exploitative as well as an act of indoctrination into ideas that are not settled but contentious, and that children will not understand. This will only encourage a young generation that seeks to report things they do not like to the police rather than seek resolutions themselves. A culture of narking has been further nurtured in Scotland where the Scottish government has produced a publicity campaign, peppering every bus with content such as:

'Dear homophobes,

We have a phobia of your behaviour. If you torment people because of who they love, shout words that we are not going to write, or use violence because you don't like someone who is holding hands with, you should be worried. If we see or hear your abuse, we're calling the police. That's because love lives in this country, not hate.

Yours,

Scotland'

It is hard to think of anything more grating than this, in terms of tone alone.

Before the lockdown, I was in a pub in Dundee and I overheard a man say 'Freddie Mercury was a great singer but a f****** queer'. The man was working class, minding his own business and giving his opinion. I was offended by his comment but felt it would have been deeply wrong to report him to the police for this. Yet this is what the Scottish government was encouraging.

The campaign in question cost £300,000. An official evaluation measured the success against a set of largely meaningless benchmarks. Its target was to 'generate 65 per cent motivation score among campaign recognisers'. Such ambition was exceeded with an actual score of 73 per cent, beyond anyone's wildest expectation, no doubt.[62] The evaluation proclaims the campaign a great success with 'spontaneous messages of thanks', and that the 'bold approach worked well to generate stand-out, recognition, motivation and word-of-mouth'. But this is delusional. The campaign generated headlines such as 'Controversial 'Dear Bigots' campaign sparks backlash', with senior politicians as well as Christian groups raising concerns.[63] It was further claimed in one newspaper that the campaign itself was reported to police as a hate crime.[64]

(Pointed?) credulity

There are examples of political as well as media credulity, verging on dishonesty. For instance, there is the case of the Polish cultural centre vandalised in the aftermath of the EU referendum, where 'xenophobic graffiti was found scrawled across the doors of the centre'.[65]

The Polish Social and Cultural Association (POSK) in Hammersmith was vandalised on 26 June 2016. The *Guardian* quoted a POSK spokeswoman as saying she did not think the incident would have happened before the referendum, but that the result had empowered a small group of extremists.[66] On the *Wikipedia* page of the organisation, it read that it was vandalised with 'racist graffiti' after the referendum.

But as noted in *Get West London*, the exact wording of

the graffiti was 'f*** you OMP'. The OMP, as it happens, is a centre-right Polish think tank which had delivered a presentation at the centre and had welcomed the referendum result – and so it is entirely possible, likely even, that the graffiti was written by a pro-remain Pole, angered by its politics.[67]

Then there was the case of the attacks on the Polish teenager in Stroud and the Asian man who intervened to help him. While widely reported as a hate crime, eventually it was treated by police as not racially-motivated.[68] And also the case of the killing of a Polish man in Harlow on 27 August 2016, widely assumed to be racist in the wake of the EU referendum, but was actually nothing of the kind.[69]

Then you have the bizarre folly of 'hate crime hoaxes', at least present in the United States. Wilfred Reilly has documented how many hate crimes that make the news, causing outrage, later transpire to be nothing of the kind, either mistakenly identified or a deliberate hoax. The motivations for such hoaxes include trying to disguise bad behaviour, making a point through something akin to 'performance art', political or financial.

Where the motivation is political, perhaps the closest comparator is diving in football, only instead of trying to gain advantage for you and your team, you are doing it for you and your group. Reilly makes the point that the 'blood libel' that Jews were attacking Christian children was an early form of hate crime hoax and that the consequences were devastating for many Jews.[70] There are no obvious British examples that spring to mind that would match some of the more infamous American cases. Nor is there any way to say, of the 100,000 recorded by police, how many are genuine – a point Reilly makes with regard to America.

But that is not to say there is not dishonesty in how hate

crime is presented, even though attacks based on hatred do occur. Take for instance an article published in the *Daily Mail Online* titled 'Shocking moment hijab-wearing girl is attacked from behind and knocked to the floor unconscious as police reveal huge rise in hate crimes against Muslims', published 7 September 2015. The article contains CCTV footage showing a man attack a young woman wearing Islamic dress. It is distressing viewing and it is claimed as an 'example of the Islamophobic offences that are on the rise in London'.[71]

This though was not an attack motivated by hostility towards Muslims. This can be found out from another article also published on the *Daily Mail Online* on 25 February 2013. The culprit, Michael Ayoade, was not charged with a religiously aggravated offence, and his actions were attributed to the victim having 'looked at him in a rude way'. Moreover, he was also convicted for an assault on another woman, whose name was not obviously typically Muslim. He had previously spent time in prison for similar unprovoked attacks against both men and women. Apparently, there was no 'psychiatric reason' for his attacks either.[72]

The reason why the 2015 article appeared was to promote a BBC documentary. It is not clear if the CCTV footage was used in the documentary or had been supplied as evidence of 'Islamophobia' by the BBC, although it did feature in other media outlets in the same context. In the same *Mail Online* article, it is claimed 'police revealed there has been a sharp rise in the number of hate crimes against Muslims in the capital'.[73] This claim is based on police recorded figures, and such numbers cannot usually be legitimately used to represent a real trend. The most important point though is that people will see the shocking footage, read the headline but not the detail, and form an opinion. This will provide ample propaganda for Islamist extremists, with which they can lure unsuspecting young men and women.

Part of the new morality is that being seen to be kind to minorities is moral, rather than treating them fairly as well as holding them to the same standards as everyone else. The first victim of this is scepticism – which is the lifeblood of honest thought. There is also the suspicion that much of this encouragement of the discourse on increasing hate crime is linked to Brexit – with the desire being to associate a democratic and legitimate decision to leave the European Union with bigotry in order to make the two synonymous. The trouble is, not telling the truth has consequences, with ordinary people making political decisions on this basis, while the lies told do not go unnoticed and only feed populism and resentment.

Coupled with this is the subjectivism of Macpherson, which states something is a hate crime if the victim says it is a hate crime, along with the injunctive that one 'believe victims'.

For example, the *Evening Standard* ran a story on 26 June 2017, under the headline: 'Muslim woman afraid to leave home after car is torched in hate crime attack'. It was reported that 'police have confirmed that they are treating the attack as a hate crime after the victim told them it was religiously motivated because she is the only Muslim living in the street.'[74] There is no reason to believe this was motivated by such hostility, even though it might seem plausible.[75]

It is a source of great frustration that so many who ought to know better, present recorded-crime statistics as evidence of a real trend. Again, this is to contravene what any first-year criminology student would learn. Typing 'rise in hate crime' into a search engine throws up the following headlines:

- 'Brexit 'major influence' in racism and hate crime rise' – BBC.[76]

- 'Rise in hate crime in England and Wales' – BBC.[77]

- 'Hate crimes are rising – but how hate is spreading is changing' – ITV.[78]

These stories from the major news broadcasters are the tip of the iceberg and are all reliant on police-recorded figures, which 'according to the ONS are not a measure of overall crime and how it has changed'.[79]

Claims of a rise in hate crime based on police-recorded figures are also repeated by politicians:

'The extent to which hate crimes have risen in recent years is shameful. It comes from the very top. Divisive, xenophobic rhetoric from politicians and leaders trickles down into abuse and violence on our streets...' – David Lammy, shadow justice minister.[80]

'... recent academic research and government data all point to the same thing: hate crimes in the UK are on the rise.' – The All-Party Parliamentary Group on Hate Crime.[81]

And by academics:

'We see the rise in hate crime as an extreme expression of a more general shift in attitudes.' – Facundo Albornoz, Jake Bradley & Silvia Sonderegger.[82]

'...and with levels of hate crime continuing to surge both within the UK and beyond...' – Neil Chakraborti & Stevie-Jade Hardy.[83]

Misrepresentation is evidenced in official inquiries and the reports of select committees and parliamentarians that rest solely on the testimonies of group-specific victim advocacy organisations.

Summary

We have an unnecessary innovation in law brought about by politicians. It has introduced inequality before the law, which only leads to more legislation. At the same time, we are seeing the innovation of extra-legal measures through the creation of 'non-crime hate incidents'. The ideas behind hate crime are imprecise, but nevertheless, hate crime practitioners believe they can proceed to bring about improvements. Key to this development is the Macpherson report, which has both damned the police unfairly and empowered activists to direct its work, away from the preferences of the average person. The government admits the problem of hate crime is abating, but nevertheless encourages the vast vested-interests that have spun up around this. No consideration is given to the damaging, unintended consequences of such action. Credulity and being seen to be virtuous take precedence over scepticism.

Fighting hate crime to 'show it has no place' in Britain is a stated policy goal. The aim is to get the numbers down but the reports up, as this shows a general improvement in the crime rate as well as supposedly increased faith in the police from minorities. At heart, this assumes the validity of the numbers in question. The next chapter looks at the empirical evidence on hate crime, as well as providing an evaluation of its validity.

2.

Evidence

Introduction

As shown in the last chapter, the government claims that hate crime is falling, although it is widely believed to be rising. How are two such claims possible? What are the evidence sources behind them?

The purpose of this section is to look at the numbers of hate crimes and the evidence sources we have for them, and to explain the reasoning behind the claim that hate crime is underreported. To reiterate, it is government policy to get the number of crimes recorded by the police up, as this is seen as reflective of trust, as well as, on Macpherson's terms, evidence of lessening institutional racism.

Numbers

Police recorded crime

The first most commonly-cited source of evidence on hate crime are police-recorded crimes. As seen in the graph below, there were 76,070 race-related hate crimes recorded by police in England and Wales in 2019/20.

This is up by 131 per cent since 2011/12. There were 6,822 religion-related hate crimes in 2019/20, up by 374 per cent over the same time frame, albeit down somewhat on the year before. The other strands are fewer in number and have also been rising.

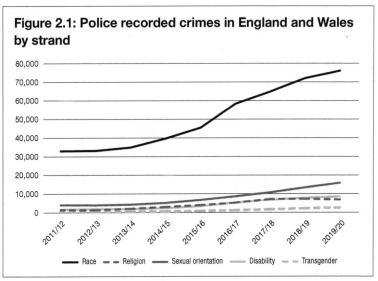

Figure 2.1: Police recorded crimes in England and Wales by strand

Source: Police recorded crime, Home Office

Police-recorded figures do not have the official status of 'National Statistics'. Moreover, it is a matter of basic criminology that recorded crime statistics cannot be used as evidence for an increase in the number of crimes, since they are subject to, among other things, the willingness to report, as well as political manipulation.

This was explained to me a few years ago by a former police-officer turned museum attendant at the Police Museum in Edinburgh. He gave an example of how homosexual offences rose at one point in the Victorian era, only to fall thereafter. This was not to do with the good people of Edinburgh becoming any more or less gay, but rather there had been a moral panic against homosexuality which was then illegal, with more calls to the police, only for it to run out of steam as people lost interest.

There are also problems with the 'flagging' of crimes as hate crimes in police databases. There is little consistency in how police keep their records from force to force. Such problems with recording hate crime were detailed at length by a report by Her Majesty's Inspectorate of Constabulary and Fire & Rescue Services. It concluded:

- Some forces were not correctly flagging offences as hate crimes.

- Even racially or religiously aggravated offences were sometimes not successfully flagged.

- The inspection found around 3,300 such offences not flagged as hate crimes.

- It reviewed 180 cases, out of which 43 had been incorrectly flagged at the time of reporting.

- It found that an audit of 700 hate crimes in one police force had concluded that as many as half of religious flags were incorrectly applied and should have been recorded as race instead.

The same review recommended a process 'whereby callers are asked why they perceive that the perpetrator has acted as he or she has done'. But to what extent would this create hate crimes out of thin air, whereby the caller comes to see a hate motivation 'now that you mention it'? Moreover, it is also made clear that the numbers are tied to budgets, and thus potentially perverse incentives:

> 'Accurate flagging of hate crime is essential so that forces and the government can understand and respond appropriately to the problem. It is also important so that PCCs and their mayoral equivalents can commission support services for victims that are appropriate to the needs of communities.'[84]

Moreover, a substantial number of hate crimes classified as 'Islamophobic' have Sikhs as victims.[85]

As seen in the table below, most recorded crimes are

public order offences, mostly offences of 'causing fear, alarm and distress'. A small percentage are serious violence involving injury – seven per cent. A strong majority do not involve violence.

Table 2.1: Hate crimes recorded by police in England and Wales – type of offence	
	%
Public order offences	53
Violence against the person with injury	7
Violence against the person without injury	14
Stalking and harassment	18
Criminal damage and arson	5
Other notifiable offences	3

Source: Police recorded crime, Home Office

What exactly is lying behind the numbers?

A freedom of information request to one police force was made, requesting a sample of around 380 cases of the specific details of what they were recording as a hate crime. While not necessarily representative, the examples give a flavour of what *may* be recorded.[86]

There are examples of crimes that would appear to be motivated by dislike of particular groups. For example:

Details	Type of hate	Location	Offence
Ip Confronted By 4 Males Who Call Ip A XXXX And Threaten To Punch And Kick Ip	Racial	Metro premises	Public disorder
Known Person Shouts Homophobic Comments Such As XXXX To Victim And Throws Glass Bottle At Victim Striking The Victims Abdomen; But Causing No Injuries. Offender Then makes Off From The Scene	Homophobic	Street	Assault without injury

Details	Type of hate	Location	Offence
2 Uk Offenders Approach Ip In Public Street Assault Who Is Visibly Jewish By Uk Means Steal Skull Cap From Ip And Make Off	Racial	Street	Assault without injury
U/K Person Spits In U/K Ip'S Face And Says 'Go Back To Yor Own Country Now We Are Out The Eu	Racial	Street	Assault without injury
Uk Person Approach Undamaged Painted Gable End Of House Using Silver Spray Paint Daub The Words 'Isis' And 'XXXX' Underneath Followed By A Swastika	Faith	Dwelling	Criminal damage – dwelling

But often many crimes are not motivated by such antipathy, but rather an argument or conflict has occurred to do with something else, which has led to terms of abuse being used that relate to the 'protected characteristics'. The motivation is to wound or gain advantage in an argument or conflict preceded by someone not receiving the treatment or things they expected:

Details	Type of hate	Location	Offence
Whilst In Public Place Ip Asked By Begger For Money Ip Refuses And Is Called abuse	Transphobic	Street	Public disorder
Known Offender Enters Polliing Station With Wrong Card Calls Ip XXXX And Makes Racist Comments To Ip	Racial	Community centre	Public disorder
Customer Who Actually Knows Manager Through An Old Associate Starts Trying To Raise Past Issues. Customer Is Asked To Leave But Becomes Racist To Mixed Race Manager Telling Him To XXXX And Calling Him XXXX	Racial	Shop	Public disorder

Details	Type of hate	Location	Offence
Known Male Enters Store Having Already Been Barred. Ip Instructs Offender To Leave Store; Offender Becomes Verbally Abusive Toward Ip; Threatening And Racial Language; Calling Ip A; XXXX Leave Scene Before Police Arrival.	Racial	Shop	Public disorder
Known Male Upon Told He Cannot Collect Medication Becomes Angry And Frustrated Leaves Store Upon Leaving Store Shouts Racial Slur At Store Workers Before Making Off Unseen	Racial	Shop	Public disorder
Civil Dispute Over Payment For Meals At Restaurant Where Customer Has Complained About Having To Wait Longer For Their Main Meals Than Is Necessary. Suspect Has Offered Payment For The Starters And Drink But Ip Has Refused Asking For The Full Amount To Be Paid Due To The Argument About The Payments The Customer Has Left And Said The Words "Go Back To Your Own Country" Which The Ip Has Perceived As Offensive And Racist	Racial	Restaurant	Public disorder
U/K Male Rings Ip And Says 'XXXX; Give Me My Phone Back'	Racial	Dwelling	Harassment
Ex Partner Of Current Girlfriend; Whilst In The Street Approaches The Ip Shouts And Swears Calling Him XXXX And Makes Threats To Stab Him And Kill Him And Then Runs Off On Police Arrival.	Racial	Street	Public disorder
Known Person Shouts 'XXXX Off' To Ip In Street During Disagreement Over Parking.	Racial	Road	Public disorder

Details	Type of hate	Location	Offence
2 Males Whilst Customers In Takeaway Shop Have Disagreement With Owner And Call Owner A 'XXXX' And Try To Discuss Brexit Politics With Owner Before Making Off. Causing The Owner To Be Distressed By The Comments Made	Racial	Shop	Public disorder
Known Male Attends Address Seeking Male Occupant Speaks With Female Occupant And Makes Threats To Put Her In Van; Rape Her And Kill Her If Male Occupant Does Not Attend To Pay Offender Money Owed To Him	Disability	Dwelling	Other violence
U/K Offender During Argument Over Return Of Goods Calls Staff Member A XXXX	Racial	Supermarket	Public disorder
During A Telephone Call; Known Friend Calls Ip A 'XXXX' Causing Her To Be Offended Due To Her Being Asian.	Racial	Dwelling	Public disorder

In some of the above cases, it is hard to infer the offender is prejudiced, otherwise why would they have entered into the social relationship in the first place? Moreover, the example immediately above is a falling-out between friends – that can be repaired by them. That the Asian woman has recourse to the police in this instance makes it both unlikely for them to reconcile or for her to have any friends in the future, since who would want to be friends with someone who reports their bad manners to the police?

Note that something as little as telling someone to 'XXXX Off' in an argument over a parking space is sufficient to for a race hate crime to be recorded. There is no evidence of racial slurs or even a crime in that example.

Some examples might be described as people trying to enforce social boundaries, through criminal measures:

Details	Type of hate	Location	Offence
U/K Male Approaches Muslim Female And Grabs Her Burka And Attempts To Rip It From Her Face Whilst Shouting 'Take That XXXX Off'	Racial & Faith	Shopping mall	Assault without injury
U/K Offender Send A Text Message To Ip Personal Mobile Phone Threatening To Do Them Harm If They Do Not Stop A Relationship With A Young Female Muslim Girl – The Ip Is A White Male	Faith	Dwelling	Harassment
During Dispute Ip Is Grabbed By The Collar And Pushed Against A Wall Who Then Says Listen Here You XXXX If You Ever Do That Again I'Ll Kill You Offender Then Makes Off	Racial	Street	Assault without injury

Other times, we are dealing with people taking offence at certain comments made and reporting them to the police. It is not obvious that these are in fact crimes and could just as easily be found on the list of 'non-crime hate incidents':

Details	Type of hate	Location	Offence
U/K Offender Uses Racist Language Causing Those Present Alarm And Distress	Racial	Street	Public disorder
Known Male Makes Verbal Comment To Ip While Passing Within Departure Terminal Of Airport. Male States Loudly 'There Goes XXXX' Causing The Ip To Feel Distressed And Offended	Racial	Airport	Public disorder
Whilst Ip Is In His Own Address; Victim Overhears The Offender Saying That The Victim And His Family Are Part Of Isis. Offender Was In His Own Garden At The Time Of The Offence	Faith	Dwelling	Public disorder
Unknown Female Customer Walks Out The Store Shouting 'Shouldn'T Be Able To Speak Their Own Language Its Wrong And Makes Me Feel Sick'; Makes Off In Unknown Direction	Racial	Shop	Public disorder

Details	Type of hate	Location	Offence
Known Person Enter Public Library And Within Sight And Hearing Of Staff Member; State; 'The Place Is Full Of XXXX.' Offender Then Asked To Leave The Library. Known Persons Then Enter Library Again On Separate Day And Make Derogatory Remark	Homophobic	Library	Public disorder
Male Offender In Sight And Hearing Of Police Shouts Racist Words	Racial	Street	Public disorder
Uk Person Use Abusive And Racially Insulting Words Presence Of The Ip Causing Her To Be Distressed In A Public Place	Racial	Bus station	Public disorder
Ip Encouters Youths In Street Who Throw Cans About And Use Abusive Language; 1 Youth Shouts '4 Eyes' Causing Ip Fear	Disability	Street	Public disorder

There are examples where children are being reported to the police for obnoxious behavour:

Details	Type of hate	Location	Offence
Whilst Playing Outside In The Street; Named Child Has Called Callers Child XXXX Causing Child To Feel Alarmed Harassed And Distressed	Racial	Street	Public disorder
Known Offenders Shout Racial Abuse At Ip And Her Son On 3 Occasions Causing Ip Alarm And Distress Abuse Used 'Go Back To Poland'; 'Get Out Of This Country'; 'You Should Be Back In Poland' And 'I Dont Want To Play With You Because You Are Polish	Racial	Street	Public disorder
Ip'S School Friend Says 'Shut Up You XXXX' To Ip Causing Alarm And Distress	Racial	School	Public disorder

There are examples of people reporting unpleasant experiences on social media, or things they have read that offend them:

Details	Type of hate	Location	Offence
Ip Converses With Offender On Facebook; Offender Makes Racist Comments Re Romanains; Latvians And Poles Causing Ip Distress	Racial	Dwelling	Harassment
Uk Person Uses Twitter To Send Offensive Not To Anyone In General Just On Twitter. Some People Have Viewed This Twitter And Has Been Brought To The Attention Of Sunderland Council Who Contact Police	Racial	Dwelling	Harassment
Known Offender Post Naked Picture Of Ip On Facebook Without Ips Consent ; Causing Harassment Alarm And Distress	Transphobic	Dwelling	Harassment

And also examples in hospitals were those involved are sometimes obviously not in their right mind:

Details	Type of hate	Location	Offence
Resident Returns From Unescorted Leave; Act Hostile And Aggressive Toward Staff; Target Ip And Threaten Violence.	Racial & Homophobic	Hospital	Public disorder
During Incident On Ward Named Offender Becomes verbally Abusive Towards Ip And Attempts To Punch Him Several Times. Offender Then Punches Ip Once In The Face And Whilst Restrained Attempts To Headbutt And Kick Ip During Assault Offender Says 'I'Ll Get You XXXX"	Racial	Hospital	Less serious violence against the person
Offender Who Is Detained Under Mental Health Act; Shouts At Another Patient Out Of Earshot 'XXXX' This Is Overheard By The Ward Nurse Who Is Alarmed By His Actions	Racial	Hospital	Public disorder

Details	Type of hate	Location	Offence
Known Offender Whilst Undergoing Treatment For Head Injury Becomes Verbally Abusive Shout Racial Slurs	Racial	Hospital	Public disorder
Known Male Whilst Patient In A Mental Health Hospital Uses Abusive Words Of Homophobic Content And Makes Threats Of Violence To Member Of Staff Whilst In Communal Areas In Front Of Other Patients.	Homophobic	Hospital	Public disorder

Some of these are *sui generis* reflecting those bizarre instances that life has a habit of throwing up. It is not obvious that prejudice or hate are involved; instead, it is clear there are other dynamics at play. That one offender has mistaken a Pakistani for a Czech would suggest we are often dealing with stupidity, not hatred:

Details	Type of hate	Location	Offence
Ex Partner Continues To Harass Ip By Setting Up Facebook Accounts In Different Names In Order To Contact Ip; Calling Him A XXXX; Also Sets Up Plenty Of Fish Accounts Under Ip'S Name; But Give It A Gay Profile; Resulting In Ip Being Contacted By Gay Men.	Homophobic	Dwelling	Harassment
Whilst Working At The Shop; Ip Stands Outside Unknown Male Says 'You Attack Children; You Go Back To Your Country To Czech Republic' Ip Says I'M From Pakistan. Offender Says 'XXXX' Spits In His Face Attempts To Hit Ip Before Leaving.	Racial	Shop	Assault without injury
Uk Offender RingsIP And Makes Derogatory Comments About The Faith Of The Vicar Stating She Is Spreading False Prophecies; Corrupting Peoples Mind And Inciting Violence. Is Abusive Towards The Vicar Then Hangs Up	Faith	Church	Harassment

Details	Type of hate	Location	Offence
2 Male Offenders Approach 3Rd Male Offender Who Is Stationary In Vehicle In Street; During Verbal Altercation Use Offensive Racist Language Towards Third Male; All Males Then Produce Weapons By Way Of Sticks And Iron Bars And Threaten Each Other In The Street	Racial	Street	Public disorder

Sometimes it is not at all obvious as to why the crime is motivated by prejudice or even how anyone could ever know what lay behind it:

Details	Type of hate	Location	Offence
Uk Person(S) Use Uk Object To Cause Damage To Outside Window Before Making Off Unseen And Unheard.	Racial	Care home	Criminal damage
Unknown Persons Enter In Victims Front Garden And Steal Solar Lights From The Garded. Enter Via Side Gate Into Rear Garden And Further Steal Property From The Rear Garden. Make Off Unseen Removing Poroperty By Unknown Means	Racial	Garden	Other theft and handling

Again, this is not a representative list of the crimes recorded, but a few general observations are offered: we are often not dealing with crimes motivated by prejudice or hatred. Rather the motivations are to do with other conflicts between individuals, whereby 'words are said'. Such conflicts are motivated by things like material desire or jealousy. Sometimes they are not even crimes.

We are seeing things recorded in which we might expect some leeway to be given, namely that the people involved are children or unwell. A result of the government's push to increase the numbers of hate crimes reported is that people are reporting things that are trivial, such as things they have seen or overheard that offend them. Likely, these are not even crimes. Every action taken by the police is at the expense of another action, since time and money are limited. Police have made all such reports a priority under elite direction that there is no place for hate crime in the United Kingdom.

In many cases, the terms of abuse do not relate to racial slurs, but are people telling others to 'go home'. While this may be offensive, in many cases such sentiments will be expressed by those of the indigenous ethnic majority who feel the terms of national belonging have been rewritten without their consent. Such sentiment has fuelled populism across the West. Is its repression through criminal law going to make it go away or, conversely, make it worse?

Often, we are seeing strange human interactions that defy classification, that are nevertheless being classified as 'hate crimes'. Numerous individuals and organisations, such as Humza Yousaf of the Scottish government, have described hate crime as 'devastating'. In many of the examples listed above, this is unlikely to be the case. Recall the argument that recording all such incidents is supposed to allow the police to measure community tensions. But in this light, it is hard to see how one can distinguish between what is random noise and what is signal.

Finally, it is apparent that a drive to increase reporting has led to too much being reported.

The Crime Survey of England and Wales

Trends in crime are instead evidenced from survey data, specifically the Crime Survey of England and Wales. This is a survey of around 40,000 households – with respondents asked to list all the crimes that occurred to them in the last year.

Across all strands, there were 307,000 in 2007/9, falling to 190,000 in 2017/20 on average per year. Race hate crimes are down from 151,000 to 104,000 in the same time frame. The trend has troughed in more recent years.[87]

Concerning religious hate crimes, the numbers seem to fluctuate without a clear trend. Crimes motivated by sexuality appear on a downward trend, as do those related to disability.

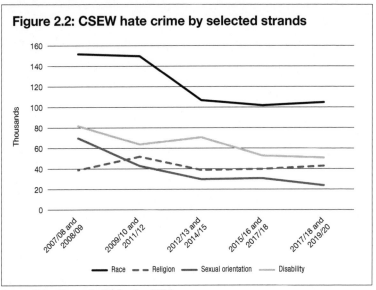

Figure 2.2: CSEW hate crime by selected strands

Source: Crime Survey for England and Wales

We believe hate crime to be underreported due to the shortfall between the Crime Survey and police-recorded figures. According to data presented by Albornoz et al. (2020), around 53 per cent of hate crimes get reported to the police, as recently as 2015/16 to 2017/18. However, the rate is roughly constant – which would imply the rise in police statistics stems from better recording not more reporting.[88]

As seen in the graph below, recorded race hate crime is converging on CSEW hate crime. This is viewed as success by the police, since there is less hate crime and the police are becoming more aware of it. However, if reporting rates are constant, it is hard to see what additional benefits there are to victims of crime that accrue from the police's better recording. Moreover, we are on track for recorded hate crime to surpass CSEW hate crime. What happens then?

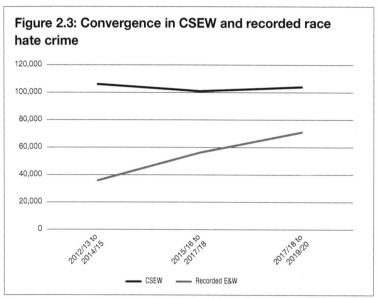

Figure 2.3: Convergence in CSEW and recorded race hate crime

Source: adapted from Home Office statistics

Spikes

The Institute for Race Relations (IRR) has written of an 'explosion of racist violence that followed the announcement of the EU referendum result'.[89] The All-Party Parliamentary Group on Hate Crime cited this research as the basis for its claim: 'The nature of the attacks was serious: characterised by physical assaults, threats to life and stabbings'.[90]

The problem with the IRR methodology is that it is based on a database of media reports. Newspapers will always tend to focus on the most extreme examples of any given phenomena, since what is newsworthy is defined as what is remarkable. But what of the actual evidence that includes all cases recorded by the police?

Spikes in police-recorded hate crime require careful consideration, in that they are likely real increases in hate crime as well as by definition, subsequent and equally real falls. They have occurred in the aftermath of 'trigger events', such as the EU referendum in 2016 and terrorist attacks.

We can judge these to be real temporary rises with subsequent falls on the basis of probability – there is no compelling theoretical reason to explain a spike otherwise. The simplest explanation is that the numbers reflect what is going on in the real world – n.b. Ockham's razor.

Figure 2.4 shows the spike in religiously or racially aggravated crimes recorded by the police around the EU referendum in 2016. Prior, the number stood at around 100 per day, peaking at 200 immediately afterwards before returning back towards its 'resting level'. It is often said that the rhetoric of pro-Leave politicians contributed towards this spike, for instance by the United Nations.[91] But such an explanation is blind to the fact that it occurred *after* the vote itself and not during the campaigning. If the country were really so responsive to political prodding, then surely any rise would have begun during the campaign.

Figure 2.5 shows the same data, only disaggregated by type of crime. Largely, the spike was accounted for by racially or religiously aggravated offences causing fear, alarm, or distress. The other more serious types of crime were both in the minority and scarcely peaked, if at all. These numbers were obtained from the Home Office by a freedom of information request.

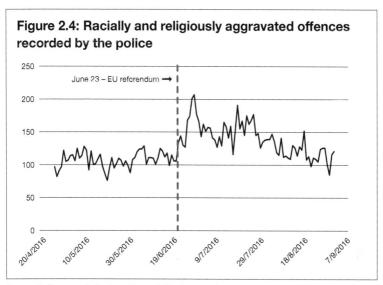

Figure 2.4: Racially and religiously aggravated offences recorded by the police

Source: Police recorded crime, Home Office Data Hub

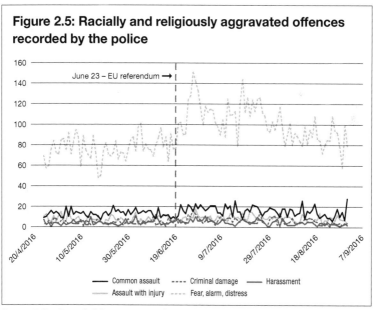

Figure 2.5: Racially and religiously aggravated offences recorded by the police

Source: Police Recorded Crime, Home Office Data Hub

However, spikes are often misconstrued as real lasting increases without statement of the subsequent decline, necessary by definition. Here, for example, is a quote from Assistant Commissioner Neil Basu, who heads the Metropolitan Police's counter-terrorism operations. He told the BBC: 'We saw a spike in hate crime after the referendum, that's never really receded.'[92]

That is factually incorrect as well as oxymoronic. You cannot have a spike that goes up but does not come down. Claims of an orgy of violence are also off the mark. Rather what we had was an outpouring of unpleasant behaviour that has not, as we shall see, manifested itself in a bulge in court prosecutions.

Long-term trends

So much can hinge on perspective – look out your window and tell me the world does not appear, on the whole, flat. The impression of a rise in hate crime stems from a rise in the numbers recorded by the police. But where numbers are presented, including by the ONS, they only show the trend from the early 2010s onwards. But what about the longer trend?

One way to do this is to look just at racially or religiously aggravated offences. Long-term data on the other 'strands' do not exist. Data are presented in the graph below.[93] Looking at this wider time series, there are two thorns in the eyes of those who seek to portray the EU referendum as having led to a lasting rise in hate crime:

- The recent rise predates the referendum, beginning in 2013.

- There was a rise between 2002 and 2006, numbers fell in the interim years.

The catch is, how come numbers rose in years long prior to the referendum? Moreover, why did they fall at precisely the point when the economy crashes, only to recover as it begins to pick up?

Were we, at the same time, getting more or less racist as a country?

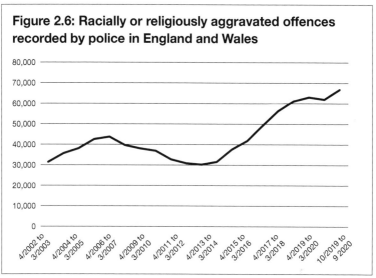

Figure 2.6: Racially or religiously aggravated offences recorded by police in England and Wales

Source: ONS

It is also worth digging into old publications. A paper from 1997 by the Political Studies Institute used the British Crime Survey, as it was back then, to estimate there were 130,000 racially motivated crimes against South Asian and black Caribbean people in 1991. This breaks down as 89,000 against South Asians and 41,000 against black Caribbean people.[94]

Using a three-wave pooled sample of the CSEW from 2016/17 to 2018/19, I was able to compute corresponding figures of 31,630 for Asian and 9,713 black people on average per year. Note that classification of ethnicity in the CSEW does not allow for distinguishing between black Caribbean and other black groups, nor South Asian from other Asian groups, but comparability is assumed, as is the comparability of methods and accuracy of measurement.

On this basis, it is estimated that in 1991 there were 60 racially-motivated hate crimes against Asian people per 1,000 and 82 against black people per 1,000. In 2016/19, the corresponding figures were eight per 1,000 for Asian and five per 1,000 for black people.

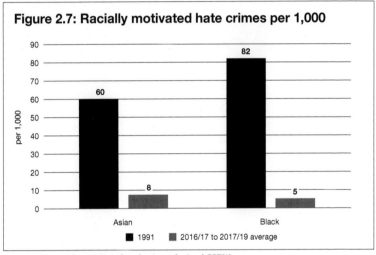

Figure 2.7: Racially motivated hate crimes per 1,000

Source: Adapted from PSI and author's analysis of CSEW

These results should be handled with caution, given the differences in classification and the time elapsed between estimates. Nor should they be particularly surprising, given crime has fallen overall at comparable rates.[95]

The courts

A third source of evidence on recent trends in hate crime are prosecutions and convictions. Such data tell you about the extent to which crimes reach the courts and are verified as such and punished. They tell you nothing about the number committed overall, nor the supply of cases going into the police and CPS.

Nevertheless, what we see in recent years is a slight decline in both the numbers of prosecutions and convictions.[96]

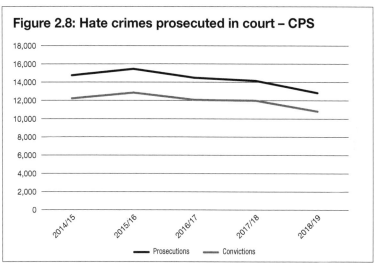

Figure 2.8: Hate crimes prosecuted in court – CPS

Source: Crown Prosecution Service (CPS), Hate Crime data

To recap, the Crime Survey says decline, the police figures say rise, the courts say (slight) decline. It is hard to find an explanation for this, although perhaps it may have something to do with public order offences, in that around half the police figures are public order offences but no more than 20 per cent of those cases prosecuted are public order offences. That greater reporting and recording do not result in greater prosecutions and convictions speaks to the failure of the policy. **The state has raised expectations of justice it has failed to deliver upon.**

Roughly 10 per cent of cases recorded by the police make it to court in the first place. Around 10 per cent of racially or religiously aggravated cases result in a charge or summons, as do nine per cent of all crimes 'flagged' as hate crimes. While around one third do not go to court because the 'victim does not support prosecution', little can be made of this since this is comparable to crimes not flagged as hate.

It has been noted that where charges are made, the victims are disproportionately police officers. Figures obtained by Melanie Newman and Richard Watson show, for instance, that West Midlands Police recorded 4,636, of which seven per cent befell a police officer. But of the 711 that were charged, 43 per cent involved a police officer as victim. The obvious explanation for this would be that the police are arresting people who then subsequently abuse them. It is easy to nick someone who is already nicked: police have the evidence and witnesses – their colleagues – and so you get disproportionate charges.[97]

Seven per cent of 4,636 offences is 325. The figures for the Metropolitan Police, four per cent out of 21,948 recorded hate crimes had a police officer as victim, or 878 offences. For West Yorkshire Police, the figures are four per cent out of 8,774 or 351 offences. These are large numbers and it is possible that the police are in effect 'gaming' the numbers reported by reporting them themselves. This would be an inevitable consequence of 'Operation Hampshire' – which is the police's policy of zero-tolerance of abuse. But as Newman pointed out, the unintended consequence of this may be that 'hate crime' comes to be seen as protection for the police at the expense of the people they police, thus undermining trust in the law.[98]

Survey evidence

The experience of hate crime, based on CSEW estimates, is rare. 1.1 per cent of Asian, 1.1 per cent of black, and 0.6

per cent of mixed-ethnic adults will be victim of a hate crime – compared to 0.2 per cent of white adults. This pales in comparison to the likelihood of being a victim of crime overall, as seen in the graph below.

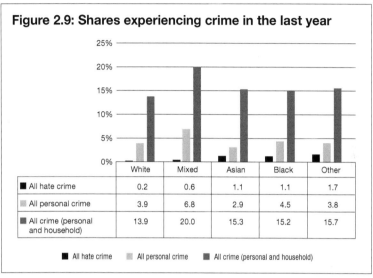

Figure 2.9: Shares experiencing crime in the last year

	White	Mixed	Asian	Black	Other
■ All hate crime	0.2	0.6	1.1	1.1	1.7
All personal crime	3.9	6.8	2.9	4.5	3.8
■ All crime (personal and household)	13.9	20.0	15.3	15.2	15.7

■ All hate crime   All personal crime   ■ All crime (personal and household)

Source: CSEW 2017/20

Another source of evidence from the Crime Survey is the extent to which people worry about being attacked on grounds of their race or ethnicity. As seen in the graph below, while the numbers are relatively stable, the shares of black and Asian people professing themselves 'very worried' is rather high – at around 13 to 15 per cent. Note that the actual chance of them being attacked is much lower, judging from the Crime Survey and, as we shall see, data from Understanding Society.

Those who contend hate crime has a wider effect on the community, creating fear, must explain how the Crime Survey can show hate crime declining but fear of it remaining constant.

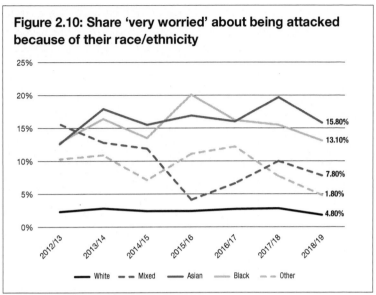

Figure 2.10: Share 'very worried' about being attacked because of their race/ethnicity

Source: CSEW author's analysis

The UK Household Longitudinal Study, known as Understanding Society, is a large-scale panel survey of households. It contains questions that ask if the respondent in the last 12 months has been:

- Insulted;
- Attacked;
- Felt unsafe; or
- Avoided places.

It also asks why, including whether any of the above were on grounds of ethnicity or religion, among other things. These data only tell us about whether a behaviour was experienced or not, and is based on the perception of the respondent. They also do not tell us anything about frequency of such occurrences.

Data from Wave 9 cover the period 2017/18. Results from an analysis of this wave are summarised below.

As seen in the graph below, 8.7 per cent of the British population (adults) experienced being insulted. However, being insulted on grounds of ethnicity or religion are rarer – 0.6 and one per cent respectively. 0.8 per cent experienced being attacked, but just 0.1 per cent both on grounds of ethnicity and religion.

Having felt unsafe is much more common – 22.4 per cent reported this. However, this is largely to do with other factors. 1.9 per cent felt unsafe on grounds of ethnicity, while 0.6 per cent felt unsafe on grounds of their religion.

Similarly, 8.6 per cent have avoided places, but just 0.5 and 0.4 per cent on grounds of their ethnicity and religion, respectively.

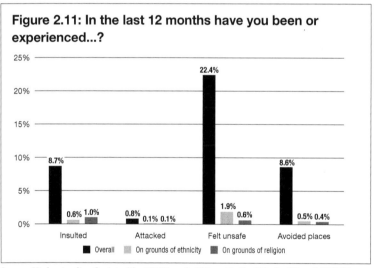

Figure 2.11: In the last 12 months have you been or experienced...?

Source: Understanding Society, The UK Household Longitudinal Study, Wave 9, 2017/18

Such figures refer to the population overall. The two graphs below show the shares affected, as broken down by broad ethnic groupings. Concerning ethnicity as grounds, Asian and black groups (including those of mixed race) report broadly comparable experiences.

Again, insults on grounds of ethnicity are experienced at a rate greater than the national average but are relatively rare – while seven per cent of Asians will experience a racial slur, most will not. Certainly, attacks by comparison are far rarer, at less than one per cent.

For whites, the comparable percentages are substantially smaller. Note that the fear of aggression on ethnic grounds is greater than actual experience of it, and this is held by a minority of black and Asian people, and not white groups.

Moreover, we should also consider opportunity to be abused – minority people will be more likely to have contact with someone from a different group who will abuse them than the other way around. However, a white person walking through a minority neighbourhood may have a comparable risk to a minority person in a majority neighbourhood. It should be added that the avoidance displayed by around five to seven per cent of black and Asian people, on grounds of ethnicity, may serve to keep whatever negative experiences they have, down.

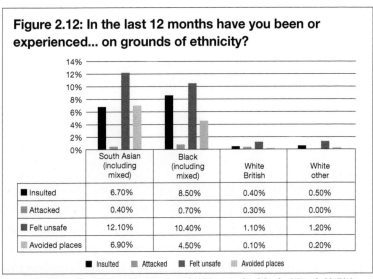

Figure 2.12: In the last 12 months have you been or experienced... on grounds of ethnicity?

	South Asian (including mixed)	Black (including mixed)	White British	White other
■ Insulted	6.70%	8.50%	0.40%	0.50%
■ Attacked	0.40%	0.70%	0.30%	0.00%
■ Felt unsafe	12.10%	10.40%	1.10%	1.20%
■ Avoided places	6.90%	4.50%	0.10%	0.20%

■ Insulted ■ Attacked ■ Felt unsafe ■ Avoided places

Source: Understanding Society, The UK Household Longitudinal Study, Wave 9, 2017/18

Concerning negative experiences on grounds of religion, the key distinction is that Asians are more likely to report this than black people, whose shares doing so are only marginally greater than white people. This may reflect the experiences of Muslims.

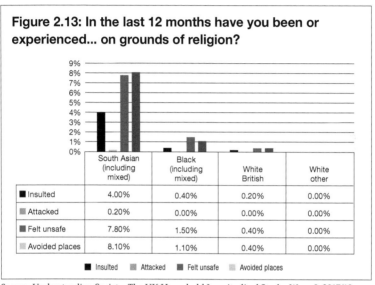

Figure 2.13: In the last 12 months have you been or experienced... on grounds of religion?

	South Asian (including mixed)	Black (including mixed)	White British	White other
■ Insulted	4.00%	0.40%	0.20%	0.00%
▨ Attacked	0.20%	0.00%	0.00%	0.00%
■ Felt unsafe	7.80%	1.50%	0.40%	0.00%
▨ Avoided places	8.10%	1.10%	0.40%	0.00%

■ Insulted   ▨ Attacked   ■ Felt unsafe   ▨ Avoided places

Source: Understanding Society, The UK Household Longitudinal Study, Wave 9, 2017/18

The same Policy Studies Institute (PSI) paper from 1997 allows us to place this evidence in historical context.[99] The paper presents nationally representative surveys of minority experiences, including the experience of racial abuse, both physical and verbal in the early 1990s. I have adapted the data presented to make them comparable with those from Understanding Society (detailed above). However, some caveats – the PSI data exclude mixed ethnic people, although there will have been substantially less in the early 1990s than there are today. Secondly, the PSI data only refers to black Caribbean people, while the data I presented from Understanding Society include all black groups. Thirdly, the

PSI data refer to 'race' as motivation, while Understanding Society data refer to 'ethnicity'.

Assuming comparability and judging from the graph below, attacks and insults are down in 2017/18 from 1993/94, although perhaps not to the extent to which we might pride ourselves. For instance, a three-percentage point reduction in the shares of South Asians reporting racial slurs directed at them over around a quarter of a century is not necessarily something to write home about.

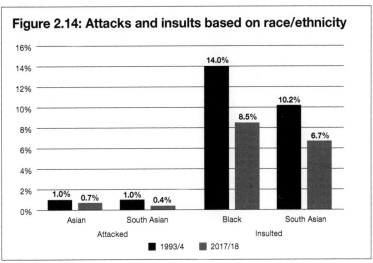

Figure 2.14: Attacks and insults based on race/ethnicity

Source: PSI, Understanding Society author's calculations.

Sexual assault

It is worthwhile to consider the Crime Survey and police recorded crime as they pertain to other types of crime. The graph below shows the number of sexual offences recorded by the police. What is most apparent is the sudden upturn in 2014. This coincides with a critical government report pointing out 'significant underreporting' of sexual offences, while Operation Yewtree, which looked into historic allegations of sexual abuse, began in 2012.[100]

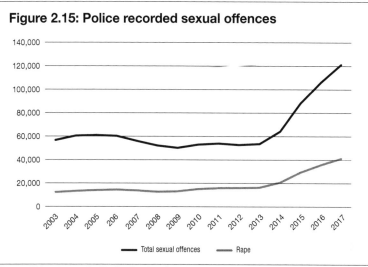

Figure 2.15: Police recorded sexual offences

Source: Crime Survey for England and Wales, 'Sexual offences in England and Wales: year ending March 2017'

At the same time, the prevalence of sexual assaults against women has been declining, as judged from the Crime Survey. The shares of women experiencing sexual assault in a given year are low, but over a lifetime, a substantial share of women will experience such a crime.[101]

Such data are important to the study of hate crime in that they show more clearly how a rise in recorded crime can come about through top-down prompting. While recorded crimes have increased, the share of women experiencing sexual assault appears to be declining, as well as low.

According to the ONS, a report by Her Majesty's Inspectorate of Constabulary and Fire and Rescue Services states that 'because of better recording standards, and compared with the findings of our 2014 inspection, forces recorded around 570,000 more crimes during 2019'. The ONS further adds: 'Prior to the coronavirus pandemic, the rate of increase had been slowing. This likely reflects the diminishing impact of recording improvements.'[102]

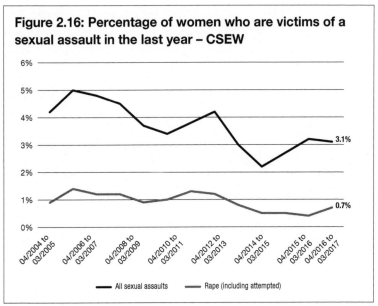

Figure 2.16: Percentage of women who are victims of a sexual assault in the last year – CSEW

Source: Crime Survey for England and Wales, 'Sexual offences in England and Wales: year ending March 2017'

Digging into the Crime Survey

The Crime Survey of England and Wales (CSEW) is fundamental to our understanding of hate crime. It is both the source of the claim that hate crime is falling and that it is underreported. As we shall see, it is also the basis for claims that hate crime hurts more, which is sometimes used to justify the special status of 'hate-motivated' crime in law. This section examines in detail the empirical evidence for such claims, as well as questioning the method in general – does it withstand scrutiny, and if not, where does that leave us?

Validity

The Crime Survey asks respondents how many crimes they have fallen victim to in the last year, and then if they thought the crime was motivated by hostility towards any of the respondent's 'protected characteristics'. If the crime is on a set list of crimes, known as CSEW crime, then it counts towards the estimate of hate crimes that is extrapolated from the sample scaled up to match the population. Estimates are derived from usually three waves, since numbers of reported crimes in the survey are small – the typical wave in recent years has only about 60 racially-motivated crimes.

Lurking away within the CSEW datafiles however, is a question that pertains just to racially-motivated crimes, and asks *why* the respondent deemed the crime to have a racial motive. Analysis of a three-wave pooled sample shows that just half are deemed racially-motivated because racist language is used. The results are presented below.

Table 2.2: Why did the respondent believe a crime to have been racially motivated? CSEW pooled 2016/19	
Racist language used (comments, abuse)	49.6%
Because of victim's country of origin	44.9%
Because of offender's race/country of origin	19.7%
Because offence only committed against minorities	8.0%
Because some people pick on minorities	11.5%
Because it has happened before	9.1%
Other	13.6%
Don't know	1.1%

Source: CSEW author's analysis

Only one of these explanations is anything like evidence of a racial motive – the presence of racist language. The others are a deduction based on the circumstances of the crime which do not reflect on what the offender's mindset actually was. That 11.5 per cent of racially-motivated hate crimes are attributed as such 'because some people pick on minorities', would point towards a 'victim mentality', although it should be pointed out that around half of such crimes in the Crime Survey befell white people.

It is also true that this shows precisely how wrong Macpherson subjectivity can be. Something is not racist just because someone says it is.

Such explorations only give us reason to doubt the level, but not the trend, presented by the Crime Survey.

Estimates for the number of hate crimes in the United States using a similar methodology are available, although the data only go as far as 2015. They were published in 2017 by the Bureau for Justice Statistics, which has not, to the best of my knowledge, provided an account of the Trump years. It was concluded that in 2015 there were 0.7 hate crimes per 1,000 persons aged 12 or above. This was not significantly different from 2004. That equates to 207,880 hate crimes in 2015.[103]

Contrast this with the most recent figure of 190,000 in 2017/20 for England and Wales. That the two figures are roughly comparable should give us pause for concern, given the huge gulf in population size. One possible reason why the American figure is lower per capita is that the National Crime Victimisation Survey is far more restrictive in what it counts as a hate crime. Crimes are only counted if they are backed up with a credible reason for a 'bias motive', namely 'hate language', 'hate symbols', or were confirmed as such by police investigators.

The recent trend is presented in the graph below. The evidence *might* suggest a drop in the number of racially-motivated hate crimes, although those classified as motivated by 'ethnicity' or religion are holding roughly steady since 2007.[104]

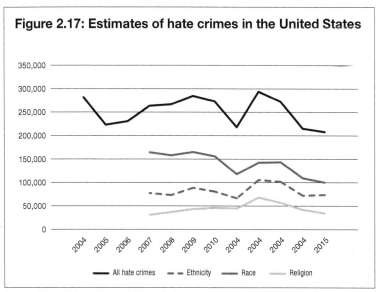

Figure 2.17: Estimates of hate crimes in the United States

Source: Adapted from National Crime Victimization Survey (NCVS)/Bureau of Justice Statistics (BJS), selected strands

If the Crime Survey is the basis for which we judge how many hate crimes ought to be reported, but that the estimate is inaccurate, or potentially too high, then it is likely we will see too much being recorded by the police.

If the Crime Survey is showing around 100,000 racially motivated hate crimes per year while there are around 70,000 recorded by police, but only half of the CSEW estimate is credible, then we have arguably already crossed the threshold into overreporting (See Figure 2.3), consistent with the qualitative evidence presented above.

Do hate crimes really hurt more?

Evidence from the Crime Survey further points to a greater emotional impact of victims of hate crime – the 'hate crime hurts more' thesis.[105] This can be used to justify their greater punishment. Results of the survey comparing victims of hate crime with all CSEW crime are presented in the table below.

The most striking thing is the stark disparity between those reporting things like fear or difficulty sleeping.

Table 2.3: Reported emotional responses of victims to a crime – CSEW

Type of emotional response experienced	All hate crime	All CSEW crime
Annoyance	48%	67%
Anger	51%	53%
Shock	47%	33%
Loss of confidence or feeling vulnerable	42%	19%
Fear	45%	17%
Difficulty sleeping	29%	13%
Crying/tears	23%	11%
Anxiety or panic attacks	34%	14%
Depression	18%	9%
Other	4%	3%

Source: CSEW 2017/20, Home Office

This does seem to be a valid claim – it is a long-standing finding within the academic literature, although an account given by Gerstenfeld presents the scholarship as often resting on small-n studies or qualitative research, and calls for more appraisal.[106] My own analysis of the Crime Survey shows the crimes classified as 'hate crimes' do tend to have a greater emotional impact, even when controlling for type of crime and injuries sustained.[107] These are emotional wounds, not the response to physical ones. It should be added that the same analysis revealed the most serious, violent crimes hurt the most.

Iganski and Lagou have written:

'… not all victims report being affected by hate crime, not all victims are affected the same way, and some victims of racially motivated crime report less of an emotional impact than some victims of equivalent but otherwise motivated crimes... Therefore, a blanked uplift in penalty in every case which rests on the offender's motivations cannot be justified if the justification for a sentence uplift is to give offenders their just deserts for the harms they inflict.'[108]

This is an important consideration. Classical notions of justice usually stress that punishment is *proportionate* to the offence, so that there is a sense of restitution for the victim. On this basis, we can argue someone who commits a crime motivated by hatred owes his victim more. But this would only hold where the damage is done, and perhaps it would be better to insist on punishment in proportion to harm than the nature of the intent behind it.

It is also often overlooked that while hate crimes may hurt more emotionally, most do not lead to the more serious forms of psychological harm – 48 per cent caused annoyance, compared to 18 per cent depression. It is a logical fallacy to justify greater punishment for hate crime on the basis it hurts more when most have no substantial psychological damage. Talk of its 'devastating' consequences is hyperbole in most cases.

Perpetrators

We speak about hate crime as though it is the work of organised racists or bigots. But as one hate crime worker put it to me, the standard incident reported to his organisation was along the lines of a row breaking out over something like a parking space, which escalated into insults. The person responsible did not set out with hatred in his heart, but rather got into a row and focused his aggression on a particular ethnic or religious characteristic of someone else.[109]

We are often told that racism on the part of those who are not white is an impossibility, since racism is an equation of hatred plus power. That there have been some notorious examples of black antisemitism in America or that Jewish racism towards blacks has also been common there would throw a spanner in the works. Who precisely is powerful here? And if the answer is to be the Jews, as one Jewish former colleague of mine would say, 'do we really want to go down that route again'?

Moreover, the courts would beg to differ, with around 14 per cent of those convicted of racially or religiously aggravated offences being non-white. Furthermore, the share of black people convicted is around double their population share, while for Asians there is a slight under-representation.

Table 2.4: Proportionality in convictions for racially or religiously aggravated offences, England & Wales 2008-18

Ethnicity	Convicted	Number	Population share (2011)
White	85.6%	30,344	86.0%
Black	5.9%	2,100	3.3%
Asian	5.1%	1,805	7.5%
Mixed	2.4%	855	2.2%
Chinese/other	1.0%	358	1.0%

Source: MoJ, Census E&W 2011

Or take these illustrative examples selected from a sample of race hate crimes recorded by the Metropolitan Police. All have ethnic minority suspects as well as victims (note that this sample of a single day's worth of hate crimes tends to fit the pattern identified above of racial slurs used during conflicts about other things, which may not even be crimes):[110]

Description of crime	Ethnicity of victim	Ethnicity of suspect
By two suspects assaulting victims and calling them racially insulting language towards the victim	Black	Arabian
By suspect who is a passenger in the victim's cab refusing to pay the fare and using racially abusive words towards the victim	Sri Lankan	Black British

Description of crime	Ethnicity of victim	Ethnicity of suspect
By victim and suspect having an argument in the street and suspect calling the victim a racially insulting name	Black	South Asian
By suspect calling victim a racially insulting name and using insulting racial phrases	Black	Black British
Suspect caught shoplifting by the victim, has called the victim a racially insulting name before throwing punches at him and being restrained by other staff and members of the public	South Asian	Black British

When we talk about racial hate crime, we always focus on white racism. Yet, the 'grooming gang' cases, as well as Islamist terrorism, are never part and parcel of the discourse on hate crime. Interviews with victims of the former often recount verbal abuse aimed at their being white and not Muslims, while Islamist terrorism is based on hatred of all who do not conform to their narrow and ignorant understanding of Islam.

Convicted perpetrators tend to be male and young while the Law Commission cites Chakraborti and Garland as saying:

'[offenders typically have] life stories characterised by deprivation, mental health problems, domestic violence, drug and alcohol issues, and patterns of criminal behaviour.'[111]

If their aggression towards those different from them is rooted in such deep trauma, it is obvious that these are not powerful individuals, but largely powerless ones lashing out. This contrasts with a BBC interview given by Paul Giannasi, who is Police Hate Crime Policy Lead at the National Police Chiefs' Council, in which he said 'hate crime is more often than not about power imbalances and is normally about the strong attacking the weak'.[112]

Moreover, this raises the question of whether or not we are

dealing with hatred, in terms of an ideological motivation at all, but rather a much wider problem of social disfunction.

Online abuse

Seemingly, every day there is a story in the newspapers about some public figure being subjected to racial or sexist slurs sent by so-called social media. But there is a risk that we fall for the fallacy of composition, whereby what is true of the experience of some fraction of the population is held to be the typical experience. While social media websites do real harm, in that they incentivise conflict as well as publish extreme views with little accountability, we should be wary of those who seek to regulate them or, at the very least, scrutinise their motivations.

Many people believe recorded hate crime statistics can be attributed to online offences. However, this is not true, with only two per cent flagged as having an online element in 2017/18, although there are doubts about data quality.[113]

Moreover, while there are real instances of sickening communications sent to figures in the public eye, they represent a small proportion of the overall number. For instance, one study found that just four per cent of tweets sent to MPs prior to the 2017 general election were abusive. It further found abuse was more likely linked to 'throwaway' accounts, specifically set up and then deleted for the purposes of abuse.[114]

Another study looked more specifically at 'hate speech' in communications sent to MPs via Twitter. Of 7.5 million replies, four per cent were abusive, with just 5,500 racist tweets. Such research utilises algorithms to classify words, and therefore struggles with nuance in meaning. In the study in question, racist abuse was defined broadly to include words such as 'shyster' and 'spiv', which are used to denote a dodgy businessman, and were broadly directed at the current prime minister, but may be taken as antisemitic when applied to Jews.

The extent to which certain MPs are abused is hard to ascertain. For instance, David Lammy received more than 1,000 racist replies – but that is 0.22 per cent of all the replies he received. For Sajid Javid, the share was 0.18 per cent, while for Diane Abbott it was 0.13 per cent. Javid and James Cleverly received about 200 racist replies each.

But the most extreme abuse – the 'N-word' – was thankfully rare. The same study found it directed abusively at Lammy 23 times, while, for Abbott, four times. Overall, it was used just 50 times to abuse MPs.[115]

Key to our judgement of abuse of public figures is proportionality, as well as the extent to which they derive benefits from social media. Studies of the nature referenced above relate just to publicly visible posts on Twitter and are based on classification of words. They do not include other social media websites or visual and private communications (direct messaging, email and so forth). Instagram and Facebook will increase the volume of abuse received, while the proportion of abusive content may be similar or not to Twitter – that is an empirical question with an empirical answer. But the evidence would suggest, in absolute terms, a lot of racial abuse is received, although, in proportional terms, the number is low.

The extent to which online 'hate speech' is experienced by the general public is not readily measured. The results of an analysis I published in a blogpost for Demos found just 1.9 per cent of internet users reported receiving abusive or threatening behaviour.[116] Online bullying seems more pronounced among children, with the ONS finding 18.7 per cent of 10 to 15-year-olds being bullied online, and 10 per cent reporting name calling. For the most part, children brush this off, since it is normal for kids to say horrible things about each other, but in extreme cases it can have devastating consequences. Also, Asian children are much less likely to experience online bullying – six per cent compared to 21 per cent of white and 18 per cent of black children.[117] Polling found that 13 per cent of whites say they have been subject to 'racist or prejudiced insults on social media', compared to 19 per cent of Pakistanis and 22 per cent of blacks.[118]

None of this provides a measure of 'hate speech' specifically directed to the 'protected characteristics' of hate crime legislation in a given year, but we can safely assume that these figures represent, at the very least, a ceiling of the amount of abuse received, irrespective of content.

We seem to lack a sense of proportionality when it comes to social media abuse. In a country of around 66 million, you will find deeply depraved individuals, while the opportunity to abuse MPs or footballers who have a bad game is open globally, as well as cheaply done. It is easy to imagine abuse conducted by hostile security services, given the furore it creates and that many abusive accounts are anonymous and set up solely for this purpose. Demands to regulate social media need to be weighed up against the benefits they bring in reaching wider audiences and breaking the establishment monopoly on mass communication. Note that the print and broadcast media has lost out heavily to social media, so it is in their interests to talk this up.

Yet, it is this sense of proportionality that seems entirely missing in our allocation of resources to this problem. For instance, in 2019 it was reported that Scotland Yard's 'online hate crime hub' had logged 1,851 incidents of online hate, with just 17 leading to criminal charges and 59 otherwise dealt with. That was at a cost of £1.7 million over two years.[119]

Summary

In this chapter I have looked at the available data sources and attempted to explain why we believe hate crime to be rising while the better evidence would point towards short-term stability and long-term decline. As a broad conclusion, we want for an accurate way of measuring hate crime, rendering policy akin to shooting in the dark.

3.

A long march through the institutions, but it's only ever a short walk to the door

I hope I have done enough in the last two chapters to convince you that the ideas behind hate crime are at least questionable and the ways in which we count it, in order to bring about a desired political goal, are flawed. I further hope that I have done enough to convince you that the kinds of identarian lobby groups that have held sway have been unhelpful as have the many, in part credulous, in part mendacious, who have encouraged them.

My thesis is that we have introduced inequality into the law which only begats more law, diverting our efforts away from where they are better spent. We treat some of the vilest criminals with new-found leniency because they are apparently now motivated by more honourable forms of malice. The courts are willing to place a higher value on life depending on the bad thoughts behind wicked deeds. Such thoughts – the *mens rea* of the offence – are now the object of punishment where they are seen to be activating crime, rather than merely a necessary component of guilt.

At root are a series of bad and new ideas imported from the United States, which has a long and inglorious record of both racial oppression and making matters worse through well intended measures that have unintended consequences. We are a country with the best history of serious thought on how to live as flawed and diverse human beings, from the English liberals, the Burkean conservatives, to the luminaries of the Scottish Enlightenment.

Yet not only have we become enthralled to bad thinking, we have nailed our morals to it, so much so that proclaiming the existence of hate crime, hate speech, structural racism, fragile whiteness and all the rest, are seen as matters of personal decency as much as statements of empirical fact. To make matters worse, as I have shown, **we have no good way to count any of this**, at least in terms of the official measurements used. How can government fight hate crime when the police recorded numbers are full of false positives, as too are the ONS estimates from the Crime Survey. We are shooting in the dark.

We live within a political ideology, namely liberalism, that allows for diversity through its ethos of live and let live. This grew out of a weariness of historic religious persecution where difference was dealt with literally by burning people to death. Yet all the time we act as though there is some better system yet to be, if only we could dream it up.

Such a way of thinking, as others have pointed out, is traceable to the French new left, postmodernism, and ultimately to the Chinese cultural revolution, as well as underlying so many other failed utopian societal projects. And yet they do seem morally plausible. That is why they catch on; the new ideas have driven out the old ideas.

There is injustice in our country, but the old ideas were always based on how we might mitigate injustice, or offer some form of restoration, rather than end it to create perfection. We are talking about the distinction between a heroic and a tragic view of human beings. History teaches us that the tragic one – that human beings are flawed but can better themselves through checks and balances on their conduct as well as a sense of humility, devotion to a task, and clear rules and boundaries – will prove more successful than radical attempts to achieve a perfectly harmonious 'New Jerusalem'.

Without the maturity to realise that there is no winning on the terms that the new ideas demand, they go unchecked. Ultimately, what has been termed the 'long march through the institutions', meaning the advance of 'new left' ideas, has been one of human beings who have been freely convinced that these are the correct approach. It is not a long march of left-wing fanatics, but rather, for the most part, the upwardly-mobile and well-meaning ordinary people, often the first in their families to attend university.

This has been encouraged by the Conservative Party, which has sought to align itself with the new thinking in order to portray itself as no longer 'nasty'. This has resulted in the selection of candidates who have little by way of intellectual training nor love of the culture that allowed this country to rise from aristocracy and mass poverty to democracy and popular home-ownership, whatever qualifications to that there may be.

There are though, in Mr Johnson's government, figures who understand what has gone wrong. They are much more in tune with the *hoi polloi*, in whose name they seek to 'level up' the country. With a strong majority in parliament, it is far past time for them to show that muscle. It is a question of both forming an intellectual argument in defence of our liberal legal tradition while also ending all state support to those who sell unwarranted victimhood.

Amidst the ranks of the 'woke', there are a great deal of decent people who only wish to help others. It is a question of convincing them that there are better ways of doing this than in stoking the cult of group victimhood. Central to this is the realisation that classical liberalism, as it is, is intended to allow for diversity. That our way of thinking is borne out of an attempt to stop religious groups from persecuting each other and to allow them to coexist. That the 'golden rule', the injunctive to live and let live, are far more successful notions to underwrite a harmonious society than 'allyship', 'decolonisation' and the anti-racism of the commissar.

But for the various vested-interests, shorter shrift is due. It may very well be a long march through the institutions, but it is only ever a short walk to the door.

Hate crime, as we approach it now, is a problem in that it fosters an image of a country at war with itself, with those deemed oppressed at the mercy of those dominant. This is far from the truth. What we have instead is peaceful coexistence and cooperation, for the most part, which we never give ourselves sufficient credit for. Always concentrating on those few negative cases, and, in doing so, committing the fallacy of composition, only serves to demoralise us. If we lose confidence in our way of life, no one is there to defend it. Off the back of this is a considerable cottage industry that fosters a false perception that only serves to lower expectations and reduce good faith.

What follows are some steps forward, both in terms of what future legislation and policy might be, as well as, statistically, how we might measure what is an important social concern in a manner that does not fuel pointless governance and bitter misunderstandings. Ultimately though, it is time for our elected politicians to stop hiding and take leadership on this issue. The proponents of identity politics have few arguments that withstand scrutiny – and it should not fall on people like Tony Sewell and his brave commission to have to point this out. Over to you Boris!

Recommendations

Legislation

It is time for a new Act of Parliament that is not to be called the 'Hate Crime Act'. Legislators will have to think of something suitable, but even to name it as such is to invite the wrong people through the door. The act should:

- Repeal all aspects of legislation that pertain to particular group characteristics;

- Define succinctly how generic hatred can be an aggravating factor, specifically where a criminal act is intended to spark wider conflict, such as terrorism, or the desecration of a sacred place. It should not look to penalise the thug who utters slurs over and above the thug who does not, nor punish merely offensive comments;

- Affirm the principle that punishment should be on the basis of harm and culpability, which can be evidenced;

- Sentence uplifts should be applied where there is ample evidence of deep or lasting psychological harm, in addition to any physical wounds;

- Provide for egregious examples of stirring up division to be prosecuted, in line with the United States Supreme Court ruling on 'fighting words';

- Prohibit the police from providing financial support to organisations that look to change the law;

- Define clearly what the police may record, distinguishing between possible crimes and intelligence, with the latter not showing up on criminal background checks; and

- Prohibit the police from taking part in political events or rallies.

Policy

- A clear statement of principle that the police are to prioritise body, then property, then feelings, and not the motivations behind a crime;

- Vexatious reports of hate crime are to be treated as wasting police time and prosecuted;

- The provision of government funding solely to organisations that provide a tangible service to victims and where there has been substantial psychological or physical trauma;

- A policy within government that advocacy groups should not be embedded in an advisory capacity on policy issues when, at the same time, they derive their income from that policy. This should not preclude organisations in receipt of public money from giving feedback on how effectively it is being spent – which would be part of any standard evaluation procedure. While we want government to listen to advice, conflicts of interest must be kept minimal;

- The government should make funding conditional on the sense that organisations are presenting statistics accurately. A code of conduct should be drawn up that precludes the lumping of specific acts of violence together with ambiguous subjective measures in order to get an inflated figure, or presenting police recorded crime figures as evidence of an actual trend, unless they can be justified as so;

- End the practice of third-party reporting – the best way to report crime is to dial 999;

- End the practice of police data-sharing on hate crime, unless the organisation in question is providing real security services;

- A general repudiation of the Macpherson review – racism is a property of individuals not institutions, unless racial inequality is explicitly defined in the rules of the institution;
- A clear statement that the police are not to intervene in situations where no crime has been committed, unless it is in the interests of keeping the peace since a little local diplomacy may go a long way;
- Replace Independent Advisory Groups with biannual town hall meetings which the press and public may attend;
- A HMICFRS investigation into Independent Advisory Groups, examining their accountability, how they are funded and who sits on them;
- The Government should reaffirm the principle of equality before the law, and that all future policy is to be made with regard to general rules; and
- A review by the EHRC into whether or not 'inclusion vetting' and the various kitemarks of diversity carried out by activist organisations actually improves things.

Statistics

- All official publications on hate crime must present Crime Survey data, showing the long-term trend first and foremost;
- Police recorded crime statistics are to be presented only as a measure of the demand placed on the police; and
- The ONS should revise the way it measures the extent of hate crime in surveys, moving away from Macpherson subjectivity and mirroring the approach taken in America of requiring credible evidence that there was a motive of hatred.

Notes

1   Fahy, P. 'Police must be careful quoting statistics when feelings are running high', *Daily Telegraph*, March 12, 2021.

2   https://www.americamagazine.org/faith/2013/11/29/windows-mens-souls

3   Jacobs, J.B. & Potter, K. (1998) 'Hate Crimes: Criminal Law & Identity Politics'. Oxford University Press.

4   Chakraborti, N. & Garland, J. (2015) 'Hate Crime: Impact, Causes & Responses'. Sage.

5   https://www.independent.co.uk/news/uk/politics/boris-johnson-westminster-insider-institutional-racism-munira-mirza-a9568456.html

6   https://assets.publishing.service.gov.uk/government/uploads/system/uploads/attachment_data/file/927673/2016_Hate_Crime_Action_Plan.pdf

7   https://www.app.college.police.uk/app-content/major-investigation-and-public-protection/hate-crime/responding-to-hate/

8   https://www.cps.gov.uk/crime-info/hate-crime

9   https://www.iclr.co.uk/knowledge/glossary/mens-rea-and-actus-reus/

10   *Daily Telegraph* 'Force apologises for saying that being offensive is a crime', February 23, 2021.

11   https://www.liverpoolecho.co.uk/news/liverpool-news/police-backtrack-after-poster-claims-19889710
As an aside, I used to work in a bar in Leamington Spa which every Sunday would host Leamington's premier/only gay night. I was told by some of the gay men, for it was only gay men who drank there, that gay men and lesbians often do not like each other. The lesbian couple, who frequently patronised the bar in the week, stayed well away from this gathering. All this talk of the 'LGBTQI+ community' is, largely, a political fiction. They do not all know each other, their group-specific interests are not all aligned; they are actually, for the most part, part and parcel of the general community.

12 https://www.gov.uk/government/statistics/an-overview-of-hate-crime-in-england-and-wales
13 https://www.hoover.org/research/sordid-origin-hate-speech-laws
14 https://www.bbc.com/news/world-europe-56181084
15 https://www.lawcom.gov.uk/project/hate-crime/
16 https://www.lawcom.gov.uk/project/hate-crime/
17 https://www.legislation.gov.uk/ukpga/1998/37/section/33
18 http://news.bbc.co.uk/1/shared/bsp/hi/pdfs/13_07_12_r_v_john_terry.pdf
19 https://www.app.college.police.uk/app-content/major-investigation-and-public-protection/hate-crime/responding-to-non-crime-hate-incidents/
20 https://www.telegraph.co.uk/news/2020/01/05/police-forces-record-thousands-hate-incidents-year-even-though/
21 https://www.standard.co.uk/hp/front/met-police-dropped-30-000-crime-reports-within-the-first-24-hours-last-year-a3931286.html
22 https://www.met.police.uk/SysSiteAssets/foi-media/metropolitan-police/disclosure_2018/january_2018/information-rights-unit---information-supplied-for-non-crime-hate-incidents
23 https://www.dailymail.co.uk/news/article-6401779/The-DOG-accused-hate-crime-fouling-outside-home-just-one-2-500-cases-probed.html
24 https://www.dailymail.co.uk/news/article-9508887/Priti-Patel-calls-police-chiefs-wipe-non-crime-hate-incidents-peoples-records.html
25 https://inews.co.uk/news/politics/nish-kumar-melanie-phillips-question-time-row-stop-and-search-racist-video-244956
26 I heard an anecdote from a man in the pub who told me that in Scotland you used to describe someone as 'coloured' if you did not know if someone was either Pakistani or Indian, for instance, and you did not wish to risk offence. He pointed out, with mirth, the lack of any real linguistic difference between 'coloured people' and 'people of colour'. He was a working-class bloke and his contempt for those who invent and enforce the distinction was obvious.
27 https://www.civitas.org.uk/content/files/MindForgdManacles.pdf
28 https://www.semanticscholar.org/paper/Profiling-Populations-Available-for-Stops-and-Miller/1005d76d353c62fcd4bf334cfd6068079f09b13d
29 https://www.civitas.org.uk/content/files/MindForgdManacles.pdf
30 https://assets.publishing.service.gov.uk/government/uploads/system/uploads/attachment_data/file/277111/4262.pdf
31 Chakraborti & Garland, op.cit.

32 https://s3-eu-west-2.amazonaws.com/lawcom-prod-storage-11jsxou24uy7q/uploads/2020/09/Hate-crime-final-summary.pdf

33 https://www.telegraph.co.uk/news/2021/02/10/offensive-comments-made-private-dinner-tables-will-not-classed/

34 https://iea.org.uk/media/the-passing-of-the-snps-hate-crime-bill-is-a-betrayal-of-the-liberal-ideals-of-the-scottish-enlightenment-says-iea-expert/

35 https://www.parliament.scot/-/media/files/legislation/bills/current-bills/hate-crime-and-public-order-scotland-bill/introduced/bill-as-introduced-hate-crime-and-public-order-bill.pdf

36 https://www.parliament.scot/-/media/files/legislation/bills/current-bills/hate-crime-and-public-order-scotland-bill/stage-3/bill-as-amended-at-stage-3.pdf

37 https://www.pressandjournal.co.uk/fp/news/politics/scottish-politics/2966266/jim-sillars-hate-crime/

38 https://www.gov.scot/groups/misogyny-and-criminal-justice-in-scotland-working-group/

39 https://www.gov.scot/publications/foi-202100150742/

40 https://www.gov.scot/binaries/content/documents/govscot/publications/foi-eir-release/2021/03/foi-202000103652/documents/foi202000103652---information-release-1/foi202000103652---information-release-1/govscot%3Adocument/FOI202000103652%2B-%2BInformation%2Breleased_Part1.pdf

41 https://www.dailymail.co.uk/news/article-9373871/Misogyny-recorded-hate-crime-government-concession.html

42 https://www.dailymail.co.uk/news/article-9508887/Priti-Patel-calls-police-chiefs-wipe-non-crime-hate-incidents-peoples-records.html

43 https://www.gov.uk/government/news/places-of-worship-protective-security-fund-open-for-applications

44 https://www.gov.uk/government/news/places-of-worship-to-get-security-funding-boost

45 https://www.justiceinspectorates.gov.uk/hmicfrs/wp-content/uploads/understanding-the-difference-the-initial-police-response-to-hate-crime.pdf

46 https://barnet.moderngov.co.uk/documents/s29145/Agenda_item_4_Hate_Crime_Third_Party_Reporting.pdf

47 https://www.whatdotheyknow.com/request/384890/response/946562/attach/html/3/Copy%20of%207740%20FOI%20Final%20v2.xls.html

48 https://www.report-it.org.uk/information_sharing_agreements

49 https://www.report-it.org.uk/files/npcc_isa_tellmama_april_2019_
final.pdf

50 A government press release reveals 'Between 2016 and 2020 we will
have provided [Tell MAMA] with £2.5 million to raise awareness
on anti-Muslim hatred and to increase reporting of hate crimes'.
https://www.gov.uk/government/news/new-process-set-out-to-
establish-a-working-definition-of-islamophobia;
According to a freedom of information request: 'In the past five
years the Home Office has awarded funding of just under £29,000
to Galop and £25,000 to Stop Hate UK for projects in the first round
of the Hate Crime Community Projects Fund (2016-17). The Home
Office also awarded Stop Hate UK £15,662 as part of 'Call 3' (2018-
19) of the Building a Stronger Britain Together (BSBT) programme.'
CST funding is a matter of public record.

51 The Community Security Trust's most recent flagship report on the
number of antisemitic incidents claims
1,668 incidents 'recorded' or 'reported to CST', but also states:
'While the decrease in Greater Manchester's figure is not
uncharacteristic of a year substantially affected by the pandemic,
the size of the fall is partly due to disruption to the flow of reports
received from Greater Manchester Police. CST's collaboration with
the police is of huge value, but the data sharing agreement is not
always a statistically consistent process.'
It is not clear to what extent the incidents the CST reports are
recorded by the police and then relayed to the organisation, and
how many come from members of the public to the CST.
https://cst.org.uk/public/data/file/7/2/Incidents%20Report%202020.pdf

52 https://www.report-it.org.uk/

53 https://www.telegraph.co.uk/news/2019/01/24/man-investigated-
police-retweeting-transgender-limerick/

54 https://www.spectator.co.uk/article/why-is-the-police-spending-
money-on-stonewall-subscriptions-

55 https://www.thamesvalley.police.uk/SysSiteAssets/foi-media/thames-
valley-police/policies/policy---independent-advisory-group.pdf

56 https://www.thamesvalley.police.uk/police-forces/thames-valley-
police/areas/au/about-us/partnerships-sponsors/what-is-an-iag/

57 https://www.thamesvalley.police.uk/SysSiteAssets/foi-media/
thames-valley-police/how_we_make_decisions/strategic-
independent-advisory-group-siag-documents---siag-meeting-
minutes-october-2020.pdf

58 https://blacklivesmatter.com/defundthepolice/

59 https://www.norfolk-pcc.gov.uk/document/1148/
    Independent-Advisory-Group-AGM-December-2020-Minutes.
    pdf?t=6c1354a91858c81a4a8a1292356c9c8cbc13c7de
60 https://policyexchange.org.uk/wp-content/uploads/2016/12/
    PEXJ5037_Muslim_Communities_FINAL.pdf
61 https://www.witneygazette.co.uk/news/19215682.hate-crime-
    awareness-competition-winner-revealed/
62 https://www.gov.scot/binaries/content/documents/govscot/
    publications/independent-report/2019/08/hate-crime-campaign-
    2018-evaluation/documents/hate-crime-campaign-2018-
    evaluation-report/hate-crime-campaign-2018-evaluation-report/
    govscot%3Adocument/Hate%2Bcrime%2Bcampaign%2B2018%2B-
    %2Bevaluation%2Breport.pdf?forceDownload=true
63 https://www.scotsman.com/regions/controversial-dear-bigots-
    campaign-sparks-backlash-76477
64 https://www.dailymail.co.uk/news/article-6255515/Hate-crime-
    posters-reported-hate-crime.html
65 https://www.theguardian.com/uk-news/2016/jun/27/brexit-polish-
    centre-london-reeling-after-graffiti-attack
66 https://www.theguardian.com/uk-news/2016/jun/27/brexit-polish-
    centre-london-reeling-after-graffiti-attack
67 http://www.getwestlondon.co.uk/news/west-london-news/polish-
    centre-graffiti-misunderstood-suggestions-11578663
68 http://www.stroudnewsandjournal.co.uk/news/15199914.VIDEO__
    Police_say_brutal_gang_attack_on_Stroud_shopkeeper_Amo_
    Singh_and_Polish_boy_was__not_related_to_race_or_ethnicity_/
69 https://www.thetimes.co.uk/article/a-polish-migrant-is-killed-
    in-harlow-essex-and-our-sneering-elite-turns-it-into-a-brexit-lie-
    phq7glps6
70 Reilly, W. (2019) 'Hate Crime Hoax: How the Left is Selling a Fake
    Race War'. Regnery Publishing.
71 https://www.dailymail.co.uk/news/article-3225020/Shocking-
    moment-hijab-wearing-woman-attacked-knocked-floor-
    unconscious-police-reveal-huge-rise-hate-crimes-against-Muslims.
    html
72 https://www.dailymail.co.uk/news/article-2284264/Michael-Ayoade-
    Thug-knocked-women-unconscious-punching-random-attacks-
    jailed.html
73 https://www.dailymail.co.uk/news/article-3225020/Shocking-
    moment-hijab-wearing-woman-attacked-knocked-floor-unconscious-
    police-reveal-huge-rise-hate-crimes-against-Muslims.html

74 https://www.standard.co.uk/news/crime/muslim-woman-afraid-to-leave-home-after-car-is-torched-in-hate-crime-attack-a3572996.html
75 My parents' car was vandalised multiple times and they are the only Scots living in his street. Are we to infer this was 'Scotophobia' or was it that they have a nice smart Mini that stood out from the other cars, prompting envy?
76 https://www.bbc.co.uk/news/uk-wales-48692863
77 https://www.bbc.co.uk/news/uk-41648865
78 https://www.itv.com/news/2020-03-02/hate-crimes-are-rising-but-how-hate-is-spreading-is-changing
79 https://www.ons.gov.uk/peoplepopulationandcommunity/crimeandjustice/bulletins/crimeinenglandandwales/yearendingseptember2020
80 https://www.theguardian.com/society/2018/oct/16/hate-crime-brexit-terrorist-attacks-england-wales
81 https://www.appghatecrime.org/publications/
82 https://www.nottingham.ac.uk/cedex/documents/papers/cedex-discussion-paper-2020-12.pdf
83 https://www.emerald.com/insight/content/doi/10.1108/SC-06-2017-0023/full/html
84 https://www.justiceinspectorates.gov.uk/hmicfrs/wp-content/uploads/understanding-the-difference-the-initial-police-response-to-hate-crime.pdf
85 https://www.pressgazette.co.uk/guardian-accused-of-self-regulation-failure-by-network-of-sikh-organisations-over-hate-crime-complaint/
86 Source: © Northumbria Police, Freedom of information (FOI) request, February 2021. Examples are quoted verbatim, typos, acronyms and all. The censorship was done by the police. I asked them not to, but they did it anyway. It should be noted these occurred in 2016 between the referendum on June 23 and August 23. They are the first 385 reported in that period. In the sample there is no particular Brexit flavour, although some ostensibly mention the referendum. Whether or not the unusual period effects the typicality of the recorded crimes, is unknown to me. What the exercise does show is what sorts of things are sufficient to be recorded as a 'hate crime'.
87 Whether the rise of 3,000 race hate crimes between the last two data points is a significant one is not known, indeed the ONS advises against hypothesis testing with these data. Note that just a couple of hate crimes reported in the CSEW would contribute to a large

number of extrapolated hate crimes, arguably consistent with what we see in the graph below. There are only about 60 race hate crimes per year in the most recent waves of the crime survey, scaling up to around 100,000 or so just an odd year, while an additional 10 cases could amount to an apparent 'rise'.

88 https://www.nottingham.ac.uk/cedex/documents/papers/cedex-discussion-paper-2020-12.pdf
89 https://irr.org.uk/app/uploads/2016/11/Racial-violence-and-the-Brexit-state-final.pdf;
90 http://www.appghatecrime.org/wp-content/uploads/2019/02/APPG%20on%20Hate%20Crime%20Report%20Hate%20Crime%20and%20Community%20Cohesion.pdf
91 https://www.bbc.co.uk/news/uk-37193140
92 https://www.bbc.co.uk/news/uk-46965780
93 https://www.ons.gov.uk/peoplepopulationandcommunity/crimeandjustice/datasets/crimeinenglandandwalesappendixtables
94 http://www.psi.org.uk/pdf/Ethnic%20Minorities%20In%20Britain_small_file.pdf
95 Between 1991 and 2017/19 crime incidents per 1,000 in England and Wales fell by 81 per cent overall compared to 93 per cent for racially motivated crimes against Asians and 88 per cent for black people.
96 https://www.cps.gov.uk/cps/publication/hate-crime-data
97 https://www.bbc.co.uk/news/uk-56546490
98 https://thecritic.co.uk/issues/may-2021/an-unfair-cop/
99 http://www.psi.org.uk/pdf/Ethnic%20Minorities%20In%20Britain_small_file.pdf
100 https://www.ons.gov.uk/peoplepopulationandcommunity/crimeandjustice/articles/sexualoffencesinenglandandwales/yearendingmarch2017
101 https://www.ons.gov.uk/peoplepopulationandcommunity/crimeandjustice/articles/sexualoffencesinenglandandwales/yearendingmarch2017
102 https://www.ons.gov.uk/peoplepopulationandcommunity/crimeandjustice/bulletins/crimeinenglandandwales/yearendingseptember2020
103 https://www.bjs.gov/content/pub/pdf/hcv0415.pdf
104 https://www.bjs.gov/content/pub/pdf/hcv0415.pdf
105 https://www.gov.uk/government/statistics/hate-crime-england-and-wales-2019-to-2020
106 Gerstenfeld, P. (2017) 'Hate Crimes, Causes: Controls and Controversies', Sage.

107 Factor analysis was conducted on the emotional harm indicators, restricted to one factor. Factor scores were computed and then regressed on hate crime, crime type, and injury sustained. Adding such controls causes the regression coefficient for hate crimes to attenuate from 1.02 to 0.72, both statistically significant (p<0.001).

108 https://journals.sagepub.com/doi/10.1177/0886260514548584

109 Insults tend to work in the following way – a focus on a prominent aspect of the individual plus a profanity. I remember once walking to college when I was younger, and someone I had known called out to me 'oi Norrie you lanky t***'. It was not that he hated tall people, he was taller than me, he just focused his aggression on an aspect of my body.

110 https://www.met.police.uk/SysSiteAssets/foi-media/metropolitan-police/disclosure_2018/march_2018/information-rights-unit---hate-crimes-recorded-by-the-mps-motivated-by-the-victims-ethnicity-and-religious-affiliation-on-4th-june-2017

111 https://s3-eu-west-2.amazonaws.com/lawcom-prod-storage-11jsxou24uy7q/uploads/2020/10/Hate-crime-final-report.pdf

112 https://www.bbc.co.uk/news/av/uk-wales-27370116

113 https://assets.publishing.service.gov.uk/government/uploads/system/uploads/attachment_data/file/839172/hate-crime-1819-hosb2419.pdf

114 https://ojs.aaai.org/index.php/ICWSM/article/view/15070/14920

115 https://arxiv.org/pdf/1910.00920.pdf

116 https://demos.co.uk/blog/behind-the-numbers/

117 https://www.ons.gov.uk/peoplepopulationandcommunity/crimeandjustice/bulletins/onlinebullyinginenglandandwales/yearendingmarch2020

118 https://assets.publishing.service.gov.uk/government/uploads/system/uploads/attachment_data/file/974507/20210331_-_CRED_Report_-_FINAL_-_Web_Accessible.pdf

119 https://www.independent.co.uk/news/uk/home-news/online-hate-crime-report-charge-sadiq-khan-a9263316.html

CIVITAS

Subscriptions and Membership (UK only)
If you would like to stay abreast of Civitas' latest work, you can have all of our books delivered to your door as soon as they are published. New subscribers receive a free copy of Roger Bootle's book, *The AI Economy: Work, Wealth and Welfare in the Robot Age* and Daniel Bentley's book, *The Land Question* on fixing the dysfunction at the root of the housing crisis. For those who would like to support our work further and get involved in our Westminster events, we have a variety of Subscription and Membership options available:
https://www.civitasonline.org.uk/product-category/subscriptions/

We regret that we are unable to post items to non-UK residents, although all of our publications are individually available via our Civitas Book Store (https://www.civitasonline.org.uk) and in most cases on Amazon.

Renewals for Existing Members

If you are an existing member wishing to renew with ease and convenience, please do select one of the subscription or membership options that most closely meets your requirements.

Make a Donation

If you like our work and would like to help see it continue, please consider making a donation. A contribution of any amount, big or small, will help us advance our research and educational activities. You can make a donation by getting in touch (020 7799 6677) or sending a simple email to info@civitas.org.uk so that we can come back to you.

Supporters of Civitas

Because we want to reach as wide an audience as possible, our subscription and membership fees are set as low as possible and barely meet printing and postage expenses. To meet the costs of producing our research and conducting our educational projects, we rely entirely on the goodwill and generosity of people who value our work.

If you would like to support our work on a rolling basis, there is a variety of advanced membership levels on offer. Supporters of Civitas have the opportunity to become more deeply engaged with the work their philanthropy makes possible.

You can pay by selecting a membership or subscription option and we will be in contact.

Alternatively, just call us on +44 (0)20 7799 6688
or email info@civitas.orguk and we can discuss your options.

If it is your preference, please make cheques payable to Civitas.

Civitas: Institute For The Study Of Civil Society
First Floor
55 Tufton Street
Westminster
London
SW1P 3QL

Email: subs@civitas.org.uk

Civitas is a registered charity, No. 1085494